SIMPLY ESSENTIAL WEDDING PLANNING KIT

Sharon Boglari

Self-Counsel Press
(a division of)
International Self-Counsel Press
USA Canada

Self-Counsel Press acknowledges the financial support of the Government of Canada through the Book Publishing Industry Development Program for our publishing activities.

Printed in Canada.

First edition: 2002

National Library of Canada Cataloguing In Publication Data

Boglari, Sharon.
Simply Essential Wedding Planning Kit

1-55180-381-X

1. Wedding—Planning. 2. Wedding etiquette. I. Title.
HQ745.B63 2002 395.2'2 C2002-910358-4

Self-Counsel Press
(a division of)
International Self-Counsel Press Ltd.

1704 N. State Street
Bellingham, WA 98225
USA

1481 Charlotte Road
North Vancouver, BC V7J 1H1
Canada

CONTENTS

CHECKLISTS

TABLE

WORKSHEETS

1 TAKING THINGS ONE STEP AT A TIME

Getting engaged and planning your wedding can be one of the most exciting times of your life. For many brides and grooms, their wedding day is a time when fantasy collides with reality in one place, on one day. From color schemes to music, to food, to your guests, every detail contributes to realizing your dream.

To make that day perfect, however, requires thoughtful and careful planning. If the two of you set priorities before you start, and openly discuss your dream — and your budget — with each other as well as your families, you can avoid stress in the weeks and months leading up to the big day.

This book is just a starting point for your imagination. The schedules and worksheets will keep you on track and give you ideas. But only you can add the personal touches that reflect your combined styles and personalities to make your day truly unique to the two of you.

Using This Guide

You've made a good start by deciding to use this book to help you make decisions and stay organized. Look over the whole book first to determine the kinds of things about which you'll need to make decisions. Next, read through the timeline in Checklist 1, then turn to the appropriate section in the book to find more details, worksheets, and checklists to help you stay on course.

Take this book with you whenever you visit wedding vendors (e.g., florists, caterers, dressmakers). By keeping all the details of your wedding in one place, you'll quickly and easily be able to lay your fingers on crucial information as you need it. And when your wedding day has passed, keep this book with your wedding album as a special memento of the fun time you had planning the wedding.

> **Wedding Wisdom**
>
> 
>
> *When planning your wedding, be open to changing your mind — but never compromise your vision.*

Getting Started

Planning your dream wedding is a lot of fun. A bride and groom can enjoy working together on many aspects of the planning, but there are also some things that you can handle separately.

Staying Organized

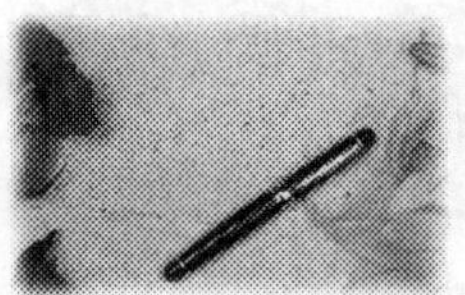

Make duplicate copies of lists to give to each other, your wedding party, and your parents.

Planning a wedding also takes time and attention to detail. Whether you have two months or two years to prepare for the event, you'll find yourself considering many of the items mentioned in the timeline set out in Checklist 1. The timeline allows for six months of planning and preparation before your wedding day. If you have less time available to you, simply adjust the timeline to focus on the areas that are important to you and that will make your wedding day uniquely yours. Use the calendar set out in Worksheet 1 to assist you.

Take things one step at a time and you won't have to worry about forgetting important details. In fact, you're sure to enjoy the months and days leading up to your wedding as much as the wedding day itself.

Eight Ways to Avoid Panic

Staying Organized

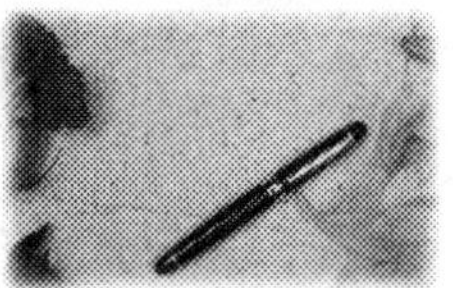

Store receipts, fabric swatches, and ideas from magazines in a folder to keep with this book.

No big event goes off without a hitch. No matter how much you plan, mistakes and delays are inevitable on the day. With some imagination and a sense of humor, you can turn these problems into stories to tell your children and grandchildren one day. Follow these tips for avoiding panic, and relax and enjoy your day.

1. Put everything in writing — from contracts with caterers to the poses you want the photographer to shoot. Don't leave anything to chance.
2. Get references from all your vendors. Speak to the people they've worked with before and make sure they are dependable and that their work is good.
3. Get extra help. Ask two or three reliable friends who are not part of the wedding party to help out on the day with last-minute details. Having a set or two of trustworthy eyes, ears, and hands will save you from frantically running around. You might consider giving each person a small gift in appreciation afterward.
4. Have a back-up plan and be prepared. If your wedding is outdoors, pick another location in case it rains. Carry an emergency kit of sewing, beauty, and medical items for those unforeseen spills, runs, and headaches. Order extra food in case Aunt Mildred forgot to RSVP but shows up anyway.
5. Don't leave anything to chance. Give maps and written directions to vendors and out-of-town guests. Allow plenty of time for decorating and for delivery of goods on the day.

6. Make sure everyone gets home safely. Appoint someone to be in charge of organizing transport at the end of the evening for guests who are drinking alcohol.
7. Be comfortable. Choose a wedding gown that allows you to move around easily and that you won't trip over when you walk up stairs or take to the dance floor. The same applies to the clothing of your wedding party. Practise walking down the aisle. It'll be one thing less to worry about on the day.
8. Make sure everyone else is prepared. Give your wedding party schedules so that they know when the photographs are being taken and haven't disappeared when you need them at the main table for the speeches.

Checklist 1

Wedding Timeline

Immediately After the Engagement

- ❑ Decide on the date for your wedding. Discuss the size and style of the occasion, and decide who will pay for what.
- ❑ Start talking to a wedding consultant if you will be using one, and make a decision as soon as possible.
- ❑ Make an appointment with the person who will perform the ceremony. Meet with your religious representative and schedule pre-marital counselling.
- ❑ Choose your ceremony and reception venues and reserve them. Start talking to caterers.
- ❑ Register at your local bridal registries.
- ❑ Choose and hire a photographer and videographer.

Six Months or More Before

- ❑ Make up your guest list.
- ❑ Find accommodation or reserve hotel rooms for out-of-town guests.
- ❑ Announce your engagement in local newspapers.
- ❑ Choose your engagement ring.
- ❑ Decide who will be in your wedding party (i.e., bridesmaids, groomsmen, and ushers).
- ❑ Choose your wedding gown and bridesmaid's dresses. Order them or hire a dressmaker to make them.
- ❑ Talk to your hairdresser, makeup artist, and manicurist and start a beauty regime for the big day.
- ❑ Select the music for the wedding ceremony and start interviewing bands or DJs for the reception entertainment.
- ❑ Decide on the style for your wedding cake and choose a baker.

Four Months Before

- ❑ Confirm guest list with caterer.
- ❑ Order or make your invitations and thank-you cards.
- ❑ Order or buy items needed for the ceremony and reception, such as napkins, table and hall decorations, floral arrangements, cake knife, toasting glasses, candles, guest book, ring pillow, and garter. Check with the caterer and the venue co-ordinator to see what they provide.
- ❑ Organize transport to the wedding and reception.
- ❑ Discuss what poses you want the photographer to shoot.
- ❑ Book a hotel room for the wedding night.
- ❑ Start planning your honeymoon. Don't forget to have a current passport and to check on visas and inoculations.

Three Months Before

- ❑ Choose and order the wedding rings, and have them engraved.
- ❑ Have both mothers co-ordinate and select their outfits.
- ❑ Choose and order tuxedos for the groom, groomsmen, and male family members.
- ❑ Meet with the florist to order the wedding flowers. Arrange to have the bride's bouquet preserved.

Two Months Before

- ❑ Mail invitations six weeks before the wedding (eight weeks for out-of-town guests). Don't forget to provide maps and written directions, if necessary.
- ❑ Arrange to have a program printed for the ceremony.
- ❑ Make hairdresser and beauty appointments for the bride and her attendants.
- ❑ Choose an outfit to wear from the reception.
- ❑ Buy gifts for the wedding party.
- ❑ Confirm accommodation for out-of-town guests.

One Month Before

- ❑ Have a final fitting for the bridal gown and bridesmaids' dresses and purchase shoes, lingerie, etc.
- ❑ Do a trial run with your hairdresser and make-up artist (do this on the same day as the bridal portrait).
- ❑ Take the bridal portrait.
- ❑ Have a bridesmaid's lunch or dinner. You can give the bridesmaids their gifts now or at the rehearsal dinner.
- ❑ Inquire with newspapers about the wedding announcement.
- ❑ Organize the rehearsal dinner. (This is usually hosted by the groom's family.)
- ❑ Decide on seating arrangements for the reception. Write out place cards and a seating map.
- ❑ Ask a friend to help at the reception with the guest book and gifts.
- ❑ Apply for your marriage license. Check whether blood tests or physical examinations are mandatory and remember to take all the required documents.
- ❑ Change your insurance policies and will to reflect your new marital status. If you have both consented to a pre-nuptial agreement, have it drawn up and signed.
- ❑ If you are changing your name, change your driver's license, Social Security Number or Social Insurance Number, bank accounts, medical plans, and credit cards.
- ❑ Fill in change-of-address paperwork.
- ❑ Start keeping a record of gifts received. Write thank-you notes for early wedding and bridal shower gifts.
- ❑ Arrange to move into your new home after you return from your honeymoon.

Two Weeks Before

- ❑ Confirm the date and location of the rehearsal and rehearsal dinner with those involved.
- ❑ Decide where the bride and her attendants will dress for the ceremony. Do a trial run. (Don't forget to break in your wedding shoes.)
- ❑ Confirm transport and parking arrangements. Have you considered access for guests with disabilities?
- ❑ Go through the whole day in your mind and consider each arrangement in detail.
- ❑ Confirm dates and arrangements with hairdresser, make-up artist, florist, photographer, videographer, caterer, and musicians/DJ.

One Week Before

- ❑ Ask someone you trust to be on hand to take care of any last-minute problems.
- ❑ Go over final details with the wedding party.
- ❑ Contact guests who have not responded and confirm final numbers with the caterer.
- ❑ Confirm honeymoon details and pack for the honeymoon. Don't forget to order traveler's checks and to pack your travel tickets.
- ❑ Indulge in some pampering at a spa and spend time with your family and friends.

One Day Before

- ❑ Attend the rehearsal and rehearsal dinner. Give bridesmaids and groomsmen their gifts.
- ❑ Give the wedding rings, marriage license, and clergy fees to the best man.

On the Day

- ❑ Have a good breakfast to see you through the day.
- ❑ Send out wedding announcements to newspapers.
- ❑ Have your hair and makeup done. Begin dressing two hours before the ceremony.
- ❑ After you've signed the marriage certificate, put it in a safe place.

After the Honeymoon

- ❑ Finish writing thank-you notes.
- ❑ Have your wedding gown professionally cleaned and stored.
- ❑ Show your photographs and wedding album to friends and family.
- ❑ Live happily ever after . . .

Worksheet 1

Calendar

Use this calendar to schedule appointments and "to do" items. Photocopy it and give it to your spouse and wedding party so that they can help you keep track.

Month of ____________						
Sunday	Monday	Tuesday	Wednesday	Thursday	Friday	Saturday

Month of ____________						
Sunday	Monday	Tuesday	Wednesday	Thursday	Friday	Saturday

Month of ______________

Sunday	Monday	Tuesday	Wednesday	Thursday	Friday	Saturday

Month of ______________

Sunday	Monday	Tuesday	Wednesday	Thursday	Friday	Saturday

2
LETTING THE WORLD KNOW YOU'RE ENGAGED

The question was popped. The answer was yes. You want the world to know.

Many couples (or their parents) choose to publish an engagement announcement in the local newspaper. You may also decide to publish one in the newspaper of your home town if you have moved away.

The engagement announcement may appear —

- immediately after the engagement,
- at the same time as the engagement party, or
- up to six or eight weeks before you are married.

Some newspapers will publish a photograph of the couple, but check what type of photograph your newspaper requires. If you want your photograph returned to you, write "Please return" on the back of the photograph and include a self-addressed, stamped envelope with your submission.

There are no rules for what to say in an engagement announcement, but some newspapers have guidelines for submitting announcements. If you're unsure what to say, contact the society editor of your newspaper to see how much detail they usually publish. Use the following examples as a starting point and fill in your own details.

> *Mr. and Mrs. H. Married of Pleasantcity, WA, announce the engagement of their daughter, Susie, to Mr. Sunny Single, son of Mr. and Mrs. N. Single of Happyville, AZ. A September wedding is planned.*
>
> *or*
>
> *Susie Single and Bert Bachelor are pleased to announce their engagement on February 14, 2001. A June wedding is planned.*

There is usually a fee for newspaper engagement announcements. Check the rates and method of payment with the editor.

Wedding Wisdom

Not sure how to word the announcement if your parents are divorced, deceased, or remarried? Consult with the social editor of your newspaper or check out one of the many books on etiquette at your local library.

3 WITH THIS RING...

If you've never bought diamond jewelry before, choosing an engagement ring can be overwhelming. But while diamonds are the traditional gem for engagement rings, many couples choose other precious stones, such as sapphires, rubies, and emeralds.

Visit a reputable jeweler who is certified by the International Gemological Institute (IGI). He or she can show you a selection of styles and diamonds, and will explain how the value of a diamond depends on a combination of the four Cs, which are cut, color, carat, and clarity:

- The **cut** of the diamond refers to the shape of the stone. The cut is essential to making the diamond sparkle. Brilliant (also called round) is the most common cut.
- The **color** of the diamond can vary from a clear white to tinges of yellow. The clearer the diamond, the more valuable it is. Jewelers use letters of the alphabet to indicate color, with A being pure white. Most jewelers will not sell any diamond rated less than J or I, as then the stone is noticeably yellow to the naked eye.
- **Carat** refers to the size and weight of the diamond. Obviously, the higher the carat the more valuable the stone. You can also buy a part of a carat. One carat is equal to 100 points. A 10-point diamond would, therefore, be one-tenth of a carat.
- **Clarity** refers to how many flaws (also known as inclusions) the stone has. Flawless stones are rare and valuable, and very slight flaws are acceptable. Most commercial diamonds have some flaws that can be seen only under magnification.

As you can see, in determining the value of a diamond you need to consider cut, color, carat, and clarity together, rather than just one of these factors in isolation. There are many choices available, and the style of the ring you choose will also influence the diamond you buy. For example, the style you choose may require a large diamond (i.e., one with a high carat weight), but you can offset the cost of that diamond by choosing one that has slight flaws not visible to the human eye (i.e., not-quite-perfect clarity). Let your jeweler guide you in finding the ring that comfortably fits both your style and your budget.

> **Being Budget-Wise**
>
> 
>
> The International Gemological Institute recommends that you spend two to three months' salary on the engagement ring. Use this as a guideline for spending, but also consider your own budget. You know best how much you can comfortably afford.

Your engagement ring is a lifetime investment. Once you have purchased a ring, have the jeweler provide you with a certificate of authenticity. You should also get a written appraisal of the value of the ring for insurance purposes. Most insurance agents recommend that you insure any valuable jewelry as separate items on your household policy.

4
MAKING A DATE

Choosing a date for your wedding can involve negotiation, compromise, and determination. You need to balance personal wishes with those of friends and family. You'll also have to consider the availability of those in the "wedding business." Like most businesses, the season or time of year can affect the availability of wedding suppliers (such as florists and caterers) and venues.

Unless you're very lucky, you probably won't please everyone. But by doing your homework and consulting with close family and friends, you and your future spouse should be able to arrive at a suitable date. Ask yourselves some of the following questions:

- Does this day fit with our personal schedules?
- Does this day fit with the schedules of our families and those in the wedding party?
- How does this day fit with our honeymoon plans? (Take into account prime-time rates in certain tourist destinations.)
- Do we have enough time to sufficiently plan the wedding?
- Does this date give us enough time to attend pre-marital counselling?
- Will our guests have to take time off work if we have the wedding on a week day?
- Will out-of-town guests have enough time to make arrangements to attend?
- Are the ceremony and reception locations available?
- Are our vendors available (photographers, hairdresser, consultants, officiant, etc.)?
- What is the likelihood of rain during this time of year?
- Is the date near to any other seasonal (e.g., Thanksgiving) or religious (e.g., Passover) holidays or popular wedding seasons (e.g., Valentine's Day)? If it is, it may be impossible to get an officiant, awkward for people to attend, or difficult to find suppliers.

Wedding Wisdom

Once you've chosen a date, don't mail the invitations until you've checked with the people who are most meaningful to you to be sure they can attend.

5 DECIDING ON THE STYLE OF WEDDING

DJ or orchestra?

Engraved invitations or e-mail?

Elvis or a pastor?

Synagogue or beach ceremony?

Receiving line or party?

The style of your wedding should be uniquely yours. You may have a large family and circle of friends and decide to rent a hotel for the day. Or perhaps you want a more intimate ceremony on your parents' front lawn. Maybe you're looking for something different for your wedding, such as a medieval-theme celebration in an ancient castle, a tropical-paradise wedding in the Caribbean, or an Elvis-style ceremony in a Las Vegas chapel. Whatever you choose should suit your personalities and lifestyle as a couple.

However, remember that this is also a day to share with family and friends, so make sure that they will be comfortable with the type of wedding you choose. Often the bride and groom (or their families) have cultural or religious traditions that they wish to incorporate into the day. Openly discuss these with both your families as well as the officiant (minister, rabbi, etc.) to make sure that everyone knows about these requests and is happy with the wedding plan.

> **Wedding Wisdom**
>
> 
>
> Read the chapter on the wedding ceremony for more information on civil and religious weddings.

There are as many different types of weddings as there are brides and grooms. If you're looking for something less traditional, consider a theme or a destination wedding.

The Theme Wedding

Some couples choose a theme for their wedding. A theme could reflect —

- the time of year (e.g., Halloween, spring)
- a color scheme,
- your cultural heritage,

- your hobbies, or
- where you got engaged or where you're going on your honeymoon.

Your theme can be as subtle or as bold as you choose. Perhaps you'll require your guests to join in and dress up, or your invitations, decorations, and food will reflect the theme. Theme weddings can be planned on a shoestring budget if necessary, with guests and dollar stores providing the atmosphere. However you do it, make sure the theme reflects your personality and that of your spouse.

The Destination or Honeymoon Wedding

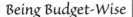

Being Budget-Wise

If you're on a tight budget, you could compromise by paying the airfare while guests pay for the accommodation.

Many couples combine their honeymoon with their wedding by having both of them in the same place. A destination wedding means that you continue celebrating your nuptials for the duration of your holiday along with your family and friends. These weddings are one way of ensuring that your guest list is limited to only your most intimate family and friends.

A destination wedding may require more organization than a smaller ceremony, and you should start planning well in advance. Remember, too, that you may be expected to pay all or part of your guests' expenses. It's only fair, after all, and it's one way to guarantee they'll show up.

Make sure you consult with your guests and check the suitability of the location with them. It may be your dream to be married in Disneyland, but some of your guests may not relish spending their summer vacation surrounded by excited children and roller coasters. Try find a destination or activity that unites you and your fiancé as well as your guests: consider skiing, scuba diving, or a cruise. If you can get your guests involved in the planning, they're more likely to enjoy themselves than if you impose a destination and time on them.

You'll probably want to invite only your closest friends and family to your destination wedding. Spending two weeks on a Caribbean beach with distant cousin Harold may be quite a different thing from just visiting with him at an afternoon reception. If possible, enable guests to stay for as long (or as short) as they like. They may choose an extended weekend or may stay with you for a full two weeks. Just make sure they have enough time to enjoy the destination as well as the wedding.

Here are some things to consider when planning a destination wedding:

- Hire a consultant who specializes in destination weddings or who works in the location of your wedding. Some resorts offer a package deal and will do some of the organization for you.
- Check your budget and the budget of your friends and family if you're not paying for them. Just because you've been saving up for two years for a wedding in Paris doesn't mean that your guests can

afford it. If you know in advance how many guests will be attending, you may be able to organize a group discount from the airline and resort.

- Work with a travel agent. Book flights and reservations early to avoid disappointment. A travel agent can handle the visa arrangements for you and your guests. Check that all your passports are current. Plan on the bride traveling in her maiden name — her passport can be updated only after the wedding.
- Plan what you will pack. If there are special items that you want at your wedding, you'll need to bring them with you. Check with your dressmaker about how to pack your wedding gown and avoid fabrics that don't travel well. Take your dress as carry-on luggage.

Finally, find out what the law requires for you to marry in another location, and get the requirements in writing from a recognized source. Will your marriage be recognized in your home country when you return? What are the legal requirements to be married in your destination? Are you allowed to conduct a religious ceremony or must it be a civil ceremony? Will you have to take any medical tests or send any documents ahead of time to get the marriage license? Is there a waiting period after getting the marriage license before you can get married? Can your family be witnesses or must the witnesses be citizens of the country in which you are married?

Staying Organized

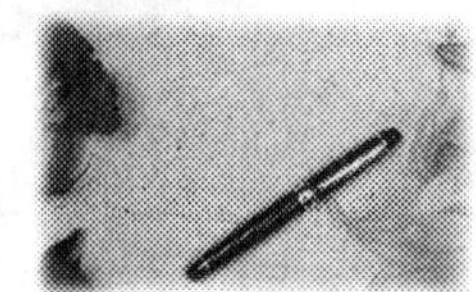

Give your guests plenty of notice for a destination wedding. They may have to re-arrange work schedules, book time off work, make travel arrangements, and find a babysitter.

6 GETTING PROFESSIONAL PLANNING HELP

Many couples turn to wedding consultants or coordinators to help them organize their big day. Perhaps the wedding is being held out of town or in one family's home town, and the couple isn't familiar with the local vendors. Often, the bride and groom are working all day and have little time available to make the necessary phone calls and visit vendors to plan the big event. Or they may be planning an exotic theme wedding and are looking for creative ideas to bring flair and style to their day.

Friends and family can play a huge role in helping out, but don't overlook the value of hiring a wedding consultant to help you orchestrate the day.

What Does a Wedding Consultant Do?

A consultant can do as much or as little as you would like him or her to do. Most professional consultants have training in the areas of event planning and management, catering, bookkeeping, and budgeting. A good consultant's experience can save you time and hassle. He or she will take you step-by-step through the planning process, telling you what to do when, and what to order from whom. You can be sure that your invitations will go out on time (and that you've included a return postcard), the DJ will be booked, and the best man will remember the rings!

A wedding consultant's contacts are invaluable when it comes to helping you stretch your dollar. A good consultant knows where to get the best deals in town on flowers and food, has experience haggling with caterers and bartenders, and can often get you good deals or extras from vendors because he or she has an established working arrangement with them.

One of the biggest advantages of hiring a wedding consultant is having an extra pair of hands around on the day. While you enjoy being the center of attention and celebrating this joyous event with friends and family, a consultant will supervise caterers, cue the speeches and music, and deal with payments and gratuities so you are free to enjoy your day. Even if you decide not to use a wedding consultant to help you plan your wedding, consider hiring one for just the day of the wedding. Your peace of mind is well worth the expense.

Staying Organized

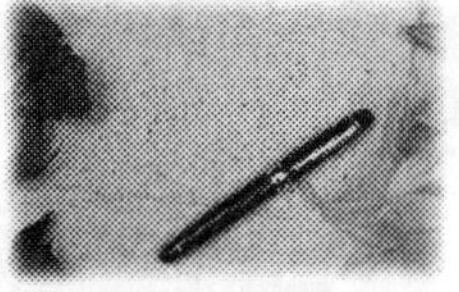

Once you've established with a wedding consultant the tasks for which each of you will be responsible, get that commitment in writing to avoid confusion or bad feelings later on.

What Does a Wedding Consultant Cost?

A consultant should be able to pass along enough savings to you to at least defray his or her own fee. Consultants may charge a flat fee, an hourly rate, or a percentage of the total cost of the wedding (usually between 15 percent and 18 percent). Ask them about any wedding packages that they offer; an experienced consultant usually has pre-negotiated deals with local venues and caterers, and if you're not picky about the location of your wedding, a package deal can save you a lot of money.

It's a good idea to first determine your budget limit and to have a rough idea yourself of what things are going to cost before talking to a consultant. That way you can see whether the consultant will be able to save you any money.

How Do I Hire a Wedding Consultant?

Start by talking to friends and getting referrals from people you know. If you are working with other wedding professionals such as florists, photographers, or caterers, or have already hired a venue, ask them if there are any local wedding consultants with whom they work well. It's important to build an effective team.

Look in the *Yellow Pages* under "wedding consultants," "bridal consultants," or "wedding planners," and check with your Better Business Bureau to make sure that the consultants you are interviewing are in good standing in your community. You will be trusting this person to help you plan an important event and spend a lot of money. Make sure you choose a certified consultant from an accredited association, and check that he or she has experience planning the size and type of wedding you have in mind.

Ann Nolan, director and founder of the Association of Certified Professional Wedding Consultants (www.acpwc.com), advises couples to interview as many wedding consultants as possible before making a decision. Don't forget to ask for references from other weddings they have planned and to interview those references as well. Most professional consultants provide a free, one-hour consultation, so take advantage of that to get to know him or her and see if you'll be able to work together.

Nolan says it's important that your personalities mesh, as you will be spending a lot of time with this person to bring your dream wedding to fruition. You'll need to trust that he or she will take responsibility for important jobs such as hiring the caterer, as well as the little things such as like remembering a cake knife. Most important, you must be able to communicate your preferences to the consultant. It's the wedding of your dreams, after all, not the consultant's.

Being Budget-Wise

Don't let a consultant sign any contracts on your behalf. Always read and understand all agreements and make sure you have the final word on any vendors he or she wants to hire.

7 WHAT IS THIS GOING TO COST?

It is crucial to decide how much you will spend on your wedding and honeymoon before you start to plan. While you don't want to go into debt for your wedding day, under-budgeting can create a disappointing experience.

You'll want to balance how you picture the perfect day with the reality of how much you can afford. If your parents are paying for part of the wedding, discuss with them their contribution and be open about your expectations for the day. Compromises are often necessary. But remember to stay focused on what's important: creating a day on which your family and friends can share in the joy of your marriage.

Wedding Wisdom

Cultural traditions may dictate who pays for what (e.g., in Chinese culture, the groom's parents are considered the hosts, and they pay for the bulk of the wedding; in Italian families, the costs are split).

Who Pays for What?

There are no rules regarding who will pay for what. These days it depends on individual budgets, who is willing, and who is financially able. You must also consider who is inviting the majority of the guests.

You may wish to use the guidelines in Table 1 to decide who will pay for what in your wedding, but remember that they are guidelines only, and may not necessarily work in your situation. Ultimately, you'll want to assign the costs based on preference and ability to pay.

Being Budget-Wise

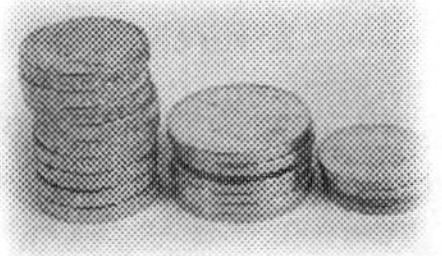

Remember, if you spend more in one area than you budgeted, you'll have to spend less on another area.

Setting a Budget

Once you've decided on a maximum amount that you can afford to spend on your wedding, make a list of your priorities for spending that money. Think about previous weddings you've attended. What do you remember the most? The food? The table decorations? The bride's bouquet? The dance music? Deciding which elements of the wedding are most important to you will help you stay focused when you're looking at wedding services. You can spend more on the things that are important to you and that your guests will appreciate and remember the most.

Many people love helping to plan for a wedding, and you may be lucky enough to have some talented (and willing) friends and family who can help

Table 1

Who Pays for What? Guidelines

Item	Bride	Groom	Bride & groom	Bride's family	Groom's family	Wedding party
Groom's wedding ring	x					
Groom's wedding gift	x					
Gifts for the bridal attendants	x					
Bridal clothing & accessories	x					
Wedding consultant	x					
Bridal lunch/dinner	x					
Bride's engagement and wedding ring		x				
Bride's wedding gift		x				
Gifts for groom's attendants		x				
Marriage license		x				
Officiant's fees		x				
Groom's clothing		x				
Boutonnieres for groomsmen		x				
Honeymoon expenses		x				
Wedding invitations and announcements				x		
Transportation of bridal party from ceremony to reception				x		
Wedding reception (including DJ/band)				x		
Flowers for ceremony, reception, bridal and bridesmaid's bouquets, corsages and boutonnieres for family		x		x		
Photography and videography				x		
Rehearsal dinner					x	
Boutonnieres and corsages for immediate family members					x	
Wedding clothing						x
Travel expenses to and from wedding location						x
Parties for the bridal couple						x

Being Budget-Wise

Keep accurate records as you progress in your planning. Take this planner with you when you go shopping. It will help you keep track of your expenses and stay on budget.

out. Perhaps an aunt can sew the wedding gown and bridesmaids' dresses. A friend may volunteer to do the flowers. Your family may pitch in to cook, and a cousin could make the wedding cake. Every little bit helps not only to enable you to spend more in other areas, but also to make your wedding truly a family event.

Use the percentages given in Worksheet 2 as guidelines for determining what percentage of your budget to spend on each item. Remember to adjust this according to your priorities and other resources. Factor in the cost of a wedding consultant if you are going to use one.

Use Worksheet 3 to determine your budgeting priorities, and then keep it updated over the next few months as you contract vendors and start spending money on your wedding. Remember, you may not use all the items on the list and there may be others that you need to add.

Worksheet 2

Budget Break-Down

Item	Typical percentage of budget (%)	My percentage of budget (%)	Notes (free items, exchanges, etc.)
Reception	50		
Clothing	10		
Photography/videography	8		
Music	7		
Miscellaneous	6.5		
Flowers and decorations	6		
Invitations and thank-you cards	5.5		
Bride's and groom's wedding rings	2		
Transportation	2		
Gifts	2		
Ceremony	1		
Total	100		

Worksheet 3

Wedding Budget

	Item	Estimated cost ($)	Actual cost ($)
Reception________%	Food		
	Drinks		
	Wedding cake		
	Venue fee		
	Wait staff		
	Rentals (Tables, chairs, glasses, cutlery, etc.)		
	Decorations		
	Other		
Clothing________%	Hair and makeup		
	Bridal gown and veil		
	Tuxedos		
	Jewelry and accessories (excluding wedding rings)		
	Shoes		
	Garter		
	Other		
Photography/ videography________%	Formal portrait fees		
	Photographer's fees		
	Videographer's fees		
	Album and reprint fees		
	Other		
Music________%	MC or DJ		
	Ceremony musicians/organist/soloist		
	Reception musicians		
	Other		
Miscellaneous________%	Rehearsal dinner		
	Marriage license		
	Taxes		
	Tips		
	Other		

Worksheet 3—Continued

	Item	Estimated cost ($)	Actual cost ($)
Flowers and decorations________%	Bouquets		
	Boutonnieres		
	Corsages for the mothers		
	Ceremony flowers		
	Reception flowers, table centerpieces, cake table, etc.		
	Other		
Stationery________%	Engagement announcements		
	Wedding invitations		
	RSVP inserts		
	Thank-you cards		
	Stamps		
	Reception napkins/matches		
	Cake boxes		
	Calligraphy		
	Other		
Bride's and groom's wedding rings________%	Bride's wedding ring		
	Groom's wedding ring		
	Other		
Transportation________%	Parking		
	To the ceremony		
	To the reception		
	From the reception		
	Guests' transportation		
	Other		
Gifts________%	Wedding favors		
	Gifts for wedding party		
	Gifts for parents		
	Gifts for each other		
	Gifts for other helpers		
	Other		
Ceremony________%	Venue fees		
	Officiant's fee or donation		
	Other		
Total			
Honeymoon			

8 THE WEDDING PARTY

Once you've decided on the style and size of your wedding, you will need to choose who will be in your wedding party. The style of your wedding will partly dictate how many wedding attendants you have. If it's a casual affair, you may have just one attendant each for you and your spouse. If it's more elaborate, you'll likely have many more attendants; after all, there will be more preparations, making more help desirable.

Unless the bride has only one sister and one best friend and the groom has only one brother and one best friend, choosing who will be in the wedding party can be a bit like negotiating a minefield. Are you obliged to ask the bride's brother be a groomsman? Should you honor a promise you made to your oldest childhood friend (with whom you've lost touch) that she would be your bridesmaid? Only you know how your family and friends may react to your choices. Just remember that these people are being chosen to support the two of you in your trip down the aisle. Make sure they are willing and able to do so.

> *Wedding Wisdom*
>
> 
>
> *It is customary to have an equal number of bridesmaids and groomsmen. But don't get too hung up on tradition. If you are close to all seven sisters in your combined families, include them all, even if you only have three groomsmen. It's your wedding, after all.*

Wedding-Party Responsibilities

Before you choose your wedding party, consider how much you will expect them to help you with your preparations. Their moral support and willingness to help you leading up to the day, as well as on it, will ensure your wedding goes smoothly. Use the following list as a starting point to help you choose who will help with what aspects of the wedding:

Maid or matron of honor

- Helps bride plan wedding and shop for gown
- Hosts a wedding shower for the bride
- Assists the bride on the day with her gown and veil
- Holds the bride's bouquet during the exchange of rings
- Holds the groom's wedding ring
- Witnesses and signs the wedding certificate
- May offer a toast at the reception

Bridesmaid

- Runs errands and helps plan the wedding
- Co-hosts wedding shower
- Assists the bride on the day with her gown and veil

Flower girl

- Carries a basket of flowers down the aisle, dropping petals or handing out single flowers as she walks

Best man

- Helps the groom with all the details of the wedding day
- Organizes a bachelor party
- Helps the groom dress and transports him to the ceremony
- Holds the bride's wedding ring
- Welcomes guests arriving at the ceremony
- Witnesses and signs the marriage certificate
- Pays the officiant his or her fee
- At the reception, makes the first toast to the bride and groom
- Organizes the car for the honeymoon and makes sure the couple's luggage is packed
- Keeps tickets, keys, and fees safe for the groom

Groomsman

- Co-hosts the bachelor party
- Ushers guests to their seats at the ceremony
- Directs guests to the reception location

Ring bearer

- Carries a satin pillow down the aisle that holds a symbolic pair of wedding rings

Members of your wedding party are usually responsible for paying for their own clothing and transportation to the wedding if they're coming from out of town. It is customary for the bride and groom to buy small gifts of appreciation for those in their wedding party.

Use Worksheet 4 to keep track of the details specific to your wedding party. Be sure to take it with you when you go shopping or for fittings, especially if some members of the wedding party aren't able to accompany you.

Worksheet 4

Wedding-Party Information

Maid or matron of honor

Name ________________________ Phone number ________________

Address ____

Dress size ________________________ Shoe size ________________

Specific duties ____

Bridesmaids

Name ________________________ Phone number ________________

Address ____

Dress size ________________________ Shoe size ________________

Specific duties ____

Name ________________________ Phone number ________________

Address ____

Dress size ________________________ Shoe size ________________

Specific duties ____

Name ________________________ Phone number ________________

Address ____

Dress size ________________________ Shoe size ________________

Specific duties ____

Name ________________________ Phone number ________________

Address ____

Dress size ________________________ Shoe size ________________

Specific duties ____

Flower girl

Name ________________________ Phone number ________________

Address ____

Dress size ________________________ Shoe size ________________

Specific duties ____

Best man

Name ________________________ Phone number ________________

Address ____

Tuxedo size ______________ Shirt (neck) __________ (sleeve) ______________

Pants (waist) ______________ (length) __________ Shoe size ______________

Specific duties ____

Groomsmen

Name ______________________ Phone number ______________________
Address ______________________
Tuxedo size ______________ Shirt (neck) ________ (sleeve) ______________
Pants (waist) ______________ (length) ________ Shoe size ______________
Specific duties ______________________

Name ______________________ Phone number ______________________
Address ______________________
Tuxedo size ______________ Shirt (neck) ________ (sleeve) ______________
Pants (waist) ______________ (length) ________ Shoe size ______________
Specific duties ______________________

Name ______________________ Phone number ______________________
Address ______________________
Tuxedo size ______________ Shirt (neck) ________ (sleeve) ______________
Pants (waist) ______________ (length) ________ Shoe size ______________
Specific duties ______________________

Name ______________________ Phone number ______________________
Address ______________________
Tuxedo size ______________ Shirt (neck) ________ (sleeve) ______________
Pants (waist) ______________ (length) ________ Shoe size ______________
Specific duties ______________________

Ring bearer

Name ______________________ Phone number ______________________
Address ______________________
Tuxedo size ______________ Shirt (neck) ________ (sleeve) ______________
Pants (waist) ______________ (length) ________ Shoe size ______________
Specific duties ______________________

9
YOU'RE INVITED TO ATTEND

Who Will Be Invited?

Rather like choosing the date of your wedding, deciding whom to invite to your wedding can involve negotiation and compromise. Very often, whoever is paying for the wedding has the final say. And again, the style and location of your wedding will determine just how many guests you can accommodate.

It helps to seek input from both families. They will know if there is a great aunt who will be mortally offended if she doesn't receive an invitation, or just how necessary it is to invite your brother's ex-wife.

Remember that not everyone you invite will be able to attend. Some couples compose two lists. List A comprises the people who must be invited; List B, the "maybes." You can mail invitations to List A at least eight weeks before the wedding, giving them a slightly earlier RSVP date. That way, if guests are unable to attend, you will still have time to invite people on List B.

Usually, only the people actually mentioned on the invitation are invited. If you want to include children, write their names on the invitation too. If you don't, it will be assumed that children are not invited. Children over 16 years should receive their own invitations. If you are inviting a guest who is single, write, for example "Pat and Guest," unless you know the name of the person's partner.

Don't forget to send invitations to your wedding attendants and their partners and to all member of your families. Yes, of course they know they're invited, but it makes a nice keepsake for them.

Staying Organized

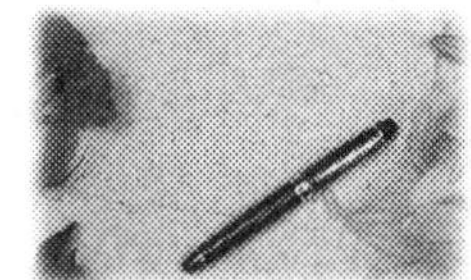

Keep your master guest list in alphabetical order. It'll be quicker and easier to find names.

Choosing the Invitations

Invitations create the first impression of your wedding. They can set the tone and style of the day. If you're having a theme wedding, they can help trigger your guests' imaginations.

Work with a printer or stationer who handles wedding invitations to come up with a design that reflects the look and feel you want the day to have. If you're ordering invitations, do so at least four months before the wedding. Order everything you need at once (e.g., invitations, response

Staying Organized

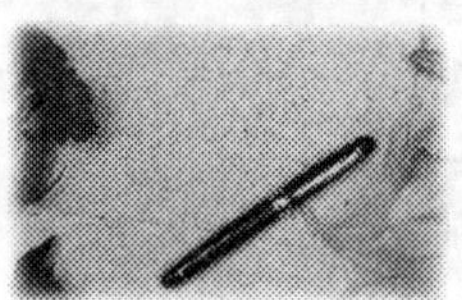

Include directions or maps with your invitations if your venue is out of town or if many of your guests are unfamiliar with the area.

cards, envelopes, and thank-you cards) to keep the costs down. Always order a few more than you'll need in case you make a mistake while addressing the invitations. With the ready availability of decorative paper these days, many couples choose to make their own invitations. It's not always cheaper, but it can be lots of fun and does add a personal touch.

What to Say

Usually the bride's parents issue the invitations, but some couples choose a more contemporary style: they issue the invitation themselves (especially if the wedding is informal and they are footing the bill).

Consult one of the many books on invitation etiquette for rules on how to word formal invitations or for invitation format if one of the parents is deceased, divorced, or re-married. A traditional wedding invitation may say the following:

Mr. and Mrs. Charles Snob
request the honor of your presence
at the marriage of their daughter
Sarah Sue Snob

to

Mr. Michael Moneybags
on Saturday, the fifteenth of June
at half past two o'clock
St. James Church
Chicago, Illinois
and afterwards at the reception
Summerhill Country Club
25 Lake Road

RSVP

Contemporary style would be less formal:

Mr. and Mrs. Fred Flower
would like you to join their daughter
Skye Flower

and

Ted Take-it-easy
in the celebration of their marriage
on Saturday, 15 June
at 2:30 p.m.
Malibu Hotel, Los Angeles
and afterwards at the reception.

RSVP

Addressing the Invitations

Formal etiquette calls for envelopes to be handwritten (preferably by a calligrapher), not typed. Use your own judgment on this; perhaps someone in your wedding party has nice handwriting, or perhaps your guests won't really care whether or not you type your envelope.

Make sure that you include a return address on the outside of the envelope in case the invitation must be returned. Ensure that you have the most up-to-date addresses and zip or postal codes for all your guests. The last thing you want is to have someone's invitation getting lost in the mail. In the United States and in Canada, post offices sell special "love" stamps for mailing. Be sure that they have the right postage for your destination, and remember that oversize or unusual shapes require more postage.

Mail invitations six weeks before the wedding (eight weeks to out-of-town guests or if you are keeping a back-up list, described above).

Wedding Wisdom

Keep a clean copy of your invitation so that you can mount and frame it or place it in your wedding album.

Keeping track of RSVPS

If you want people to respond promptly, make it easy for them. Print a telephone number on the invitation or include a self-addressed and stamped response card (make sure it has enough postage if you are inviting guests from outside the country). Here's a sample of a response card:

The favor of a reply is requested by 30 May

M ________________________________

will/will not attend

Keep track of who has replied by using Worksheet 5. Bear in mind that if you end up with more or fewer people than you had anticipated, you may have to make adjustments to the size of your hall and your catering service.

Worksheet 5

Guest List

Guest list: Bride

Name	Address and phone number	Date mailed	Reply received	Number of guests	Gift received	Thank-You sent

Worksheet 5—Continued

Guest list: Groom

Name	Address and phone number	Date mailed	Reply received	Number of guests	Gift received	Thank-You sent

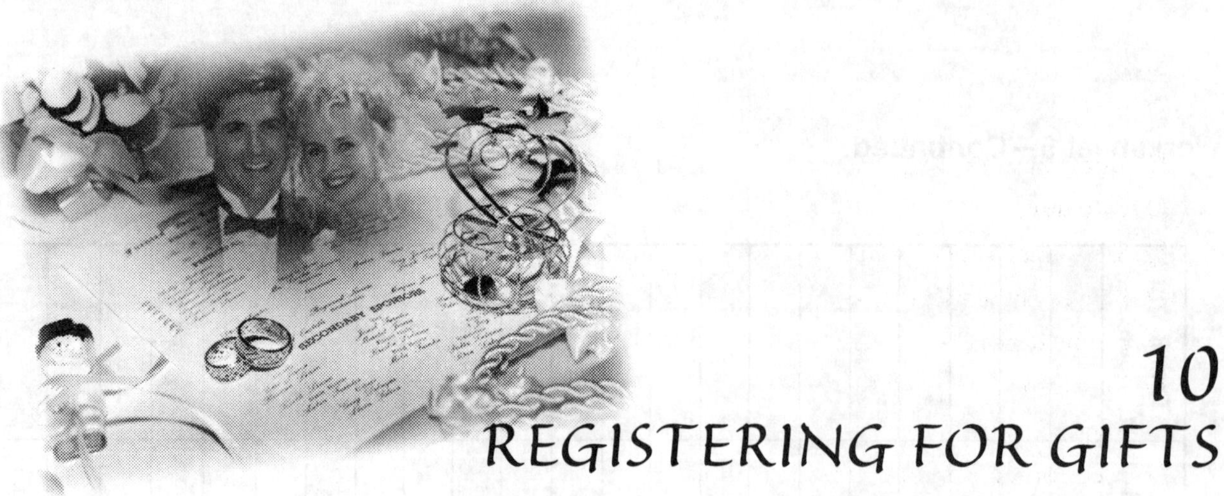

10
REGISTERING FOR GIFTS

Even if you think you already have all you need for your home, don't overlook the benefits of a gift registry. Registering for gifts not only ensures that you get the items you need in the color and style you like, but also often makes buying a gift easier and less stressful for your guests. In addition, it means you're less likely to receive duplicates or to have to make exchanges.

When deciding for which gifts to register, consider your lifestyle as well as how much and the kind of entertaining you do. Think about your decorating style and the colors you prefer. Make a note of the size of your linens and pay attention to how much space you have in your home to store or use the gifts.

Use Worksheet 6 to make a list of gifts for which you've registered and to mark them off when you receive them. Make a point of offering a variety of price points to suit everyone's budget (there's no need to record the actual prices; recording the price range will allow you to see at a glance whether you have enough variety). Pick a store (or no more than three stores) that is within easy reach of most of your guests. If you choose more than one store, register for different things at each to avoid receiving duplicate gifts. Most national department stores allow out-of-town guests to choose a gift at a local branch or through the Internet.

Register early to give your guests ample time to shop, then let them know via word of mouth (i.e., through your families and wedding party) where you've registered.

The following are some ideas for registry items:

- Formal dinnerware
- Informal dinnerware
- Crystal and glassware
- Serving pieces
- Bathroom linens
- Bedroom linens
- Table linens
- Luggage

Wedding Wisdom

You're not limited to registering for china or towels. Some couples opt for a honeymoon or mortgage registry. Guests place money on deposit with a travel agent or deposit funds into an interest-bearing mortgage account. (See Chapter 24 for more on honeymoon registries.)

- Cookware
- Bakeware
- Small appliances
- Knives and cutlery
- Home decor
- Furniture
- Major appliances
- Electronics, cameras, etc.
- Sports goods
- Gardenware

If the maid of honor hosts a wedding shower for the bride, use Worksheet 7 to keep track of the gifts received, and update your gift registry if necessary.

Worksheet 6
Gift Registry

Gift	Store	Price range ($-$$$)	Received from	Thank-you sent

Worksheet 7

Wedding Shower

Hosted by ______________________________

Date ______________________ Time ______________________

Place ______________________________

Theme ______________________________

Guest	Gift	Thank-you sent

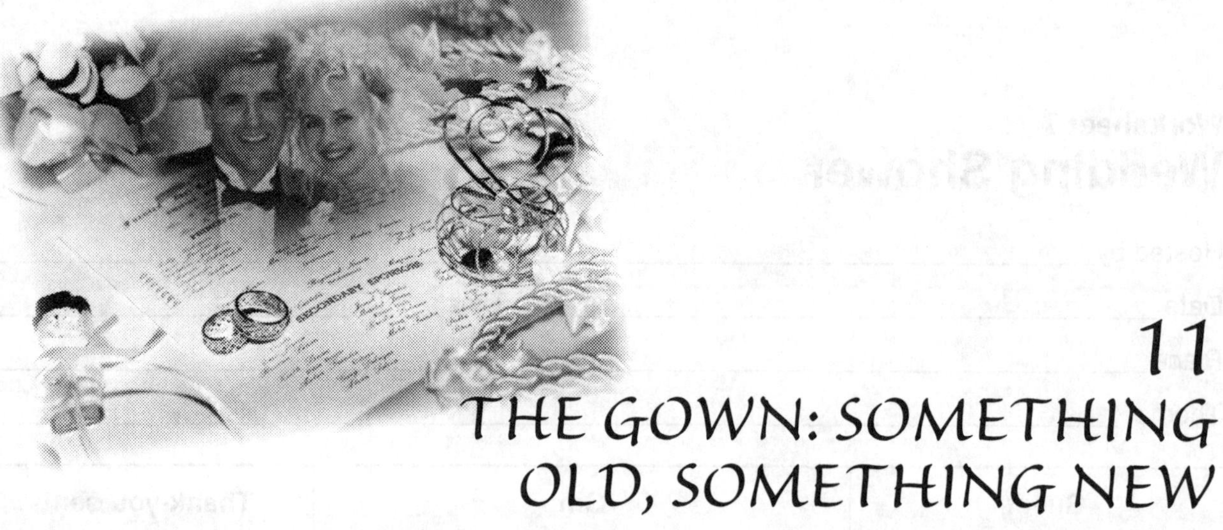

11
THE GOWN: SOMETHING OLD, SOMETHING NEW

For many brides, their wedding gown is the incarnation of a dream. Fantasy combines with reality to make them feel like a princess for a day. The bride's gown often sets the style for the wedding, and if you're having a theme wedding it's the perfect place to start.

"Today's brides realize that their gown should match their personality," says Sandra Sung, who custom designs gowns for brides across the world and also sells her designs in retail stores in Canada and the United States. "The gown plays a large part in making the bride look and feel beautiful and special, but it's important that the focus is on the bride." Sung says that the bouquet, veil, hair, and jewelry all contribute to the final look — as will a radiant smile and a happy bride. Most important, she says, is that the bride feels comfortable in and enjoys her gown throughout the day.

The season and location of your wedding, as well as how formal it is, will affect your choice of the color and the style of your gown, train, and veil. If you are having a religious ceremony, check whether or not there are any restrictions on your gown (and those of your bridesmaids). For example, if you are not allowed to have bare shoulders during the wedding ceremony, you could wear a shoulder wrap for the ceremony and remove it for the reception.

> **Wedding Wisdom**
>
> 
>
> *If you are visiting a bridal salon, call ahead to make an appointment. This will guarantee you receive one-on-one attention.*

Searching for the Perfect Gown

Sandra Sung advises brides to start looking for a gown at least four months before the wedding. Even if you immediately find the perfect gown, you may need to order it in your size and will probably need at least one fitting. For a custom-designed gown, you may have to allow time to have the fabric ordered.

Scour magazines, department stores, and dress patterns for ideas. It's a good idea to shop with your mother or a friend, but try not to involve too many people as you may find yourself confused by a plethora of different tastes and opinions.

Don't limit yourself to large department stores or bridal salons. Many brides have found their perfect gown in vintage and consignment stores.

Check whether a family member has kept her dress in storage for such an occasion. If you're trying to cut costs and don't mind wearing someone else's dress, try a rental agency. And contrary to what you might believe, having a gown custom designed can often be less expensive than buying one off the rack, especially if the gown must be altered to fit you.

Check whether the retailer or designer requires a deposit and when the final payment is due. Make sure you are clear on the store's exchange and cancellation policies, and whether there are extra charges for fittings.

Use Worksheet 8 to keep track of the details of your wedding gown.

Avoiding Mothballs

Many brides choose to keep their gowns after their wedding days. Perhaps you want your sister or daughter to wear it one day, or you plan to renew your wedding vows in it 25 years from now. Or you may just want to be able to put it on every few years and feel like a princess again. Whatever your reason for keeping your gown, it is imperative that you store it properly so that it remains in the same condition as when you first wore it as a bride.

Sandra Sung recommends you have your gown professionally cleaned after you have worn it for your wedding. A professional cleaner will place the gown in a special box, which you should store sealed in a dry closet.

Certain fabrics and styles will store better than others, so if you intend to store your gown, discuss this with the designer or sales assistant. Choose a style that has clean lines and good fabric for storage. Sequins and beading can tarnish and mark the gown. If your gown has these decorations, you should remove them before storing it.

Wedding Wisdom

If you've bought new shoes to match your gown, be sure to wear them in well. You wouldn't want to miss out on the fun because of sore feet! If you've chosen heels, wear them to all your gown fittings and practise walking in them while wearing your gown and train so that you are confident walking down the aisle.

Attire for the Wedding Party and Families

The bride's choice of gown and the couple's preference usually influence what the wedding party wears. While you want the wedding party's clothing to complement the style of your wedding, remember that they usually pay for their attire, so try to stay within their financial limits. You should also consider whether or not they will want to wear their clothing again to other smart functions.

It's usually best to consult with those in the wedding party to get their input on their attire. They need to feel comfortable in what they are wearing; otherwise, they may not be much help to you on the day!

When choosing your bridesmaids' gowns, take into consideration their personalities, age, coloring, and body shape. Their clothing needn't be identical to one another. As long as their attire is similar in style and color, they could each wear something slightly different, yet unique.

Worksheet 8
Bridal Gown

Gown

Designer ______________________ Style number ______________ Size ________

Description ____

Date ordered ______________________ Approx. cost ______________________

Deposit ______________________ Balance due ______________________

Retailer ______________________ Phone ______________________

Salesperson ____

Delivery date ____

Fitting date(s) ____

Alteration costs ____

Headpiece/veil

Designer ______________________ Style number ______________________

Description ____

Date ordered ______________________ Approx. cost ______________________

Deposit ______________________ Balance due ______________________

Retailer ______________________ Phone ______________________

Salesperson ____

Delivery date ____

Shoes

Designer ______________________________ Size ______________________

Description ____

Date ordered ______________________ Approx. cost ______________________

Retailer ______________________ Phone ______________________

Salesperson ____

Costs for dyeing ____

Delivery date ____

Other accessories

	Date purchased	Where	Cost
Bra			
Slip			
Stockings			
Gloves			
Garter			
Handbag			
Jewelry			
Ring pillow			

For the men, choose clothing that fits the formality and style of the bride's gown and the wedding. Try to rent tuxedos or suits from the same shop so that they look identical.

Last, but not by any means least, are the mothers. Have them check with each other to ensure that their dresses complement each other and the wedding party. (This attention to detail will be particularly evident in your wedding photos.) It is the mother of the bride's prerogative to choose her outfit first, and she should do so as early as possible to give the mother of the groom enough time to find hers.

Use Worksheet 9 to record what your wedding party will wear.

Staying Organized

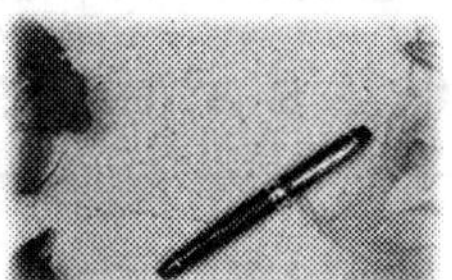

If your bridesmaids need to have their shoes dyed to match their gowns, try to have all the shoes dyed at the same place. Doing so will ensure a good match.

Worksheet 9

Wedding Party Attire

Bride's attendants

	Description	Cost	Store
Maid/matron of honor Color Fabric Size			
Bridesmaids' dresses Color Fabric Sizes			
Flower girl's dress Color Fabric Size			
Shoes Style Color Sizes Dyeing charge			
Accessories Hat Gloves Other Fittings and alterations			
Mothers Style Color			

Worksheet 9—Continued

Groom's attendants

	Description	Cost	Store
Groom Style Color Size			
Best man and groomsmen Style Color Sizes			
Ring brearer Style Color Size			
Fathers Style Color Sizes			
Shoes			
Fittings and alterations			

12
SAY IT WITH FLOWERS

Flowers are one of the easiest ways to transform a bare room into a magical reception venue. From boutonnieres and corsages to flower girls' baskets and confetti, from aisle runners and altar arches to centerpieces and cake decorations, few weddings occur without a trip to the florist. And of course, no bride's dress is complete without her bouquet.

Flowers can also be the undoing of many a carefully planned wedding budget. Work closely with a reputable florist you trust to select flowers that match both the look you're trying to achieve for your wedding and your budget. Try these ideas or come up with your own creative ones:

- Try to work with flowers that are in season. Importing out-of-season flowers from across the world can be pricey.
- Choose only a couple of different types of flowers. The more variety you have, the more they'll cost.
- Stick with a single style for all the bouquets and arrangements. Apart from giving your wedding a more unified look, it makes life easier for the florist. Avoid elaborate arrangements that are time-consuming to produce.
- Double up how your flowers are used. Flowers from the church can be transported to the reception. Bridesmaids' bouquets can be used to decorate the cake and gift table.
- Consider limiting flowers to the wedding party only, but beware of offending mothers who may expect to be wearing a corsage.
- Pick a few focal points in the reception area and focus on those. Remember that your guests will spend more time at the reception than at the ceremony, so put most of your effort there.
- Use flowering plants as table decorations. They'll continue blooming long after the wedding is over and provide a lasting memory of your special day.
- Rent large potted plants and shrubs to decorate your reception area. They provide a natural setting and can be less expensive than elaborate floral arrangements.

Use Worksheet 10 to keep track of the flowers you have ordered and their cost.

Staying Organized

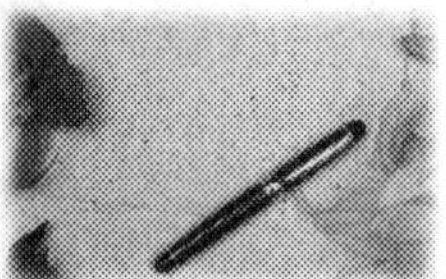

A bridal consultation with a florist can last at least one hour. Be courteous to the florist and make an appointment before visiting or visit during non-peak hours or seasons.

Working with a Florist

Many florists will charge a consultation fee, so the more prepared you are when you visit them the better. Have a clear picture in your mind of the ceremony and reception locations. If possible, bring photographs or have the florist visit the sites in person so that he or she can see how they look and will know how much time to allow for setup. Give the florist swatches of your gown and those of your bridesmaids so that he or she can try match, or at least complement, your color theme.

Have an idea of the kinds of flowers and styles you like and how much you are prepared to spend. Try to keep an open mind. A good florist will work within your budget and will suggest creative solutions for replacing expensive out-of-season flowers with those that are in season to help you meet your budget.

Staying Organized

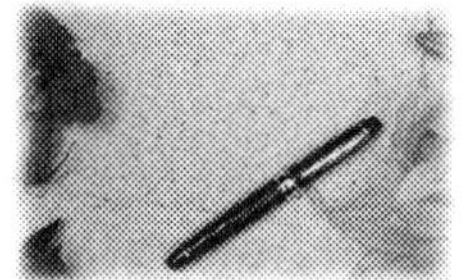

If a florist is arranging your flowers on site, give him or her a map or clear directions for getting there.

Preserving Your Bouquet

Some brides decide to press their bouquet or make potpourri from the petals. If you want to preserve your whole bouquet, speak to the florist who designed it. He or she can give you the best advice for the kinds of flowers in your arrangement. Usually, you will need to remove the moisture from the flowers and spray them with a protective spray. A good way to remove the moisture is to place the bouquet in a box and cover it in silica gel for at least a week.

Wedding Wisdom

If you want to keep the bride's bouquet as a memento, considering ordering a smaller, separate bouquet to use in the bouquet toss.

Worksheet 10

Flowers

Florist ______________________________

Contact ______________ Phone ______________

Cost ______________ Taxes ______________

Deposit ______________ Balance due ______________

Delivery time ______________

Set-up time ______________ Disassemble time ______________

Directions to venue given ______________

	Description	Number	Cost
Bouquets			
Bride			
Maid/matron of honor			
Bridesmaids			
Flower girls			
Bride's toss bouquet			
Hair			
Bride			
Maid/matron of honor			
Bridesmaids			
Flower girls			
Boutonnieres			
Groom			
Best man			
Groomsmen			
Father of bride			
Father of groom			
Other family			
Corsages			
Bride's mother			
Groom's mother			
Other family			
Rehearsal dinner			
Bride's corsage			
Mothers' corsages			
Table centerpiece			
Ceremony			
Altar			
Chuppah			
Aisle runner			
Main entrance			
Pew markers			
Flower petals for tossing			
Reception			
Centerpiece: main table			
Centerpiece: other tables			
Decorations for cake table, guest book, buffet table			
Venue decorations			

13 MEMORIES

Choosing a Wedding Photographer

Long after your wedding day is over, you'll look back on your wedding photos to remember your special day. That's why it's important to choose a professional photographer. A good photographer does more than operate a camera and snap some pictures. The difference between a professional and an amateur photographer lies in the ability to capture the magic and emotion of the day.

Start your search for a photographer at other weddings you attend. Notice how the photographer gets his or her shots. Can he or she almost invisibly capture the intimate moments of the wedding, or is the photographer constantly in the way of guests? You can also look in the *Yellow Pages,* call a professional photographers' association in your area, or check out your city's annual bridal show for referrals.

Once you've narrowed your search to two or three photographers, check out their references and take a look at their portfolios. A professional photographer should be able to show you not just a variety of photographs from different weddings, but also all the photographs from at least one entire event. This way you'll be able to see how the photographer handles a variety of shots throughout the day — not just his or her best shot of the day.

Wedding Wisdom

In the United States, consult the Professional Photographers of America (PPA) at <www.ppa.com>. In Canada, consult the Professional Photographers of Canada (PPOC) at <www.ppoc.ca> for photography referrals.

Interviewing a Wedding Photographer

Professional photographer Mike Guilbault, of Photogenics, The Art of Photography, in Ontario (www.mgphotography.com), says it is essential that you meet a prospective wedding photographer in person. He suggests you use your initial contact (usually by telephone) to ask general questions about the photographer's availability and price range, and also to arrange to meet the photographer in person so that you get a better "feel" for him or her. You want to be able to work with the photographer and have confidence in him or her during a very exciting, but also very stressful day.

Guilbault suggests you ask the photographer the following questions during the interview. By asking these questions, your photographer will

Wedding Wisdom

Your wedding photos should tell a story — from the moment you put on your dress, through the ceremony, the cutting of the cake, and right up until you leave the reception. Look for a photographer who can capture the personality of your event.

know that you've done your research and are a well-informed consumer. Go with your instinct and choose by personality as much as photographic style.

1. **Are you a full-time photographer?** There are many part-time photographers and some of them do nice work. The question really is if you want to trust your wedding memories to someone other than a true professional. (A professional photographer by definition of the Professional Photographers of Ontario is someone who earns the majority of their income through photography.)
2. **Are you a member of a professional photography association?** Although one doesn't have to belong to an association to be a good photographer, many associations require their members to be full-time photographers, and some require that their members pass a qualification before allowing them to advertise that they are members. Membership in such an organization, although not necessary, shows that the photographer is at least serious about his or her craft. In some organizations, a photographer can become accredited for particular genres of photography, such as weddings and portraits.
3. **What equipment do you use?** This isn't as important now as it used to be. There are many fine 35 mm cameras around, and digital photography is making great inroads in day-to-day photography. Many photographers will use a variety of cameras, from 35 mm to medium-format equipment such as Hasselblad or Mamiya. The quality obtained from medium-format, however, is far superior to 35 mm, and the images are much sharper and have greater depth. A photographer who has invested in medium-format equipment is quite serious about photography.
4. **How much time do you spend at a wedding?** This will partly be determined by the packages the photographer offers. Some photographers start at the beginning of the day and stay with you well into the evening. Most cover the four basic locations of bride's home (before the ceremony), ceremony, park or studio for formal family groups, and, finally, reception. Usually, if the photographer is staying for the entire reception, it will cost you more.
5. **What's included with the package?** There are as many packages and ways to produce a wedding album as there are photographers. Some will include only the bridal album, while others include plenty of extras. It really depends on what you want, and often a photographer will create a package to suit your needs.
6. **What style of photography do you shoot?** This is getting into the heart of the photographer and is the most important reason why you should choose a particular photographer. Do you like candids and casual photography or do you prefer the more traditional and posed images? Many photographers will offer both, but you should view

their samples to see if their style suits your personality. You can do this only by visiting the photographer; shopping by phone doesn't work. A new trend is purely candid, photo-journalistic wedding photography, frequently done without flash and very often in black and white. Done well, it can be striking and dramatic and can create a great story line in your wedding album. But make sure the samples you see tell a story and are not just snap shots!

7. **Do you use an assistant?** An assistant isn't necessary. But a photographer who uses an assistant has more time to spend with you and concentrate on capturing the essence of your wedding — not worrying about where he or she left that last roll of film.
8. **Do you have a backup location?** While most couples prefer outdoor scenery for their wedding photography, what happens if it rains? Does the photographer have a studio large enough to handle your wedding party and other relatives that need to be included in your photos? Is it air-conditioned? In July, that could be important!
9. **Do you have a wedding-photography contract?** A contract not only protects the photographer, but also protects you. In addition, it will provide you with details about payments, delivery, dos and don'ts, and other conditions important to the success of your wedding photography.
10. **How much time is needed for the photography?** You need to know this ahead of time so you can plan for your wedding-day schedule to include the photography. It's not fair to hire the photographer for a job such as this and not give him or her the required time to work. If you're an hour late from the hairdresser, don't expect your photographer to be able to capture all the images you want or the variety you anticipated. Good work needs time.

Once you've decided on a photographer and have discussed the fees, reserve him or her as early as you can. The best photographers are booked up months in advance.

> **Wedding Wisdom**
>
> 
>
> *It's currently popular to leave a disposable camera on each table at the reception for guests to take shots. Apart from getting your guests involved in creating memories for your wedding, it also gives you shots from a different perspective than that of the professional photographer.*

Getting the Shots You Want

Many couples give the photographer a list of the poses they absolutely want (see the suggested list in Checklist 2) and then leave the rest up to the photographer. You may consider giving a copy of the list to a close friend who is not part of the wedding party and asking him or her to attend the photo sessions to make sure that the photographer gets everything on the list. That friend can also be a valuable resource for identifying people to the photographer so that an important family member isn't missed because the photographer didn't know what he or she looks like.

Formal Portraits

If you have the budget, you may decide to have a formal portrait taken before the wedding. This could be a portrait of the bride alone or of the bride and groom together. The formal portrait usually takes place a few weeks before the wedding, and often accompanies the wedding announcement on the day of the wedding.

The portrait is usually done in the photographer's studio, and for the bride, is often less stressful than trying to fit in formal photographs of her gown on the day of the actual wedding. Of course, you may still take photos on the day, but you'll likely be far more relaxed knowing that you already have beautiful photographs that were taken under controllable situations. Check whether a formal portrait is part of your photographer's package.

When you go in for your formal portrait, make sure that every aspect of your gown is identical to how it will be on the day of your wedding. It's a good idea to have your portrait done on the same day as you have your practice run with your hairdresser so that your hair and hair accessories (veil, etc.) match, too.

Album

When you receive your photographs after the wedding, you'll want to protect them from dusty and greasy fingers as you show them to your friends and family. Photographs are shown to their best advantage in an album. Some photographers will arrange the album as part of their package. However, scrapbooking is popular these days, and can provide evenings of activity for a new couple arranging photos and wedding mementos in a meaningful way in their wedding album. If you're not sure where to start, check out the calendar at your local community college. Many of them offer scrapbooking or photography-framing courses.

Choosing a Videographer

Much of the advice given for choosing a photographer applies to choosing a videographer for your wedding. Get the best you can afford and check out his or her work before hiring. When viewing samples of the videographer's work, check to see which features of the samples are included in his or her price. Special effects often cost much more and are not always included in the quote. These are some other things to check out:

- What format is the videographer using? VHS is the lowest-quality format, while digital is the highest.
- Does the videographer have back-up equipment?
- Where will the microphone be placed during the ceremony so that it will pick up the vows?

Checklist 2

Photographic Poses

Rehearsal

Arrival time ______________________ Departure time ______________________

Location ______________________

Before the ceremony

Location ______________________

Arrival time ______________________ Departure time ______________________

- ❑ Bride dressing/fixing hair and makeup
- ❑ Bridesmaids helping bride dress
- ❑ Bride with her mother
- ❑ Bride with her father
- ❑ Bride with both parents
- ❑ Bride with grandparents
- ❑ Bride with siblings
- ❑ Bride with matron of honor
- ❑ Bride with bridesmaids and flower girl
- ❑ Groom in his tuxedo
- ❑ Groom with his mother
- ❑ Groom with his father
- ❑ Groom with both parents
- ❑ Groom with grandparents
- ❑ Groom with siblings
- ❑ Groom with best man
- ❑ Groom with groomsmen and ring bearer
- ❑ Parents/wedding party receiving flowers/boutonnieres

At the ceremony

Location ______________________

Arrival time ______________________ Departure time ______________________

- ❑ Ushers escorting guests to seats
- ❑ Bride's mother being seated
- ❑ Groom's family being seated
- ❑ Seating of other special guests
- ❑ Groom at the altar with best man and attendants
- ❑ Bride and father entering the ceremony location
- ❑ Procession down the aisle with bridesmaids and flower girl
- ❑ Bride and father coming down the aisle
- ❑ Bride's father giving bride's hand to the groom
- ❑ Bride and groom saying their vows
- ❑ Bride and groom lighting unity candle
- ❑ Ring exchange
- ❑ The kiss
- ❑ Signing the marriage certificate
- ❑ The recessional
- ❑ Bride and groom leaving the ceremony location
- ❑ Bride and groom getting into the car

Before the reception

Location ____________________

- ❑ Bride and groom with the officiant
- ❑ Bride and groom's hands
- ❑ Bridesmaids looking at bride's ring
- ❑ Bride with bridesmaids
- ❑ Bride and groom
- ❑ Groom with groomsmen
- ❑ Bride with her parents
- ❑ Bride and groom with maid of honor and best man
- ❑ Bride and groom with wedding party
- ❑ Bride and groom with all parents
- ❑ Bride and groom with all family (including siblings)
- ❑ Bride and groom with bride's family
- ❑ Bride and groom with groom's family
- ❑ Bride and groom looking at each other

At the reception

Location ____________________

Arrival time ____________________ Departure time ____________________

- ❑ Bride and groom arriving at reception
- ❑ Receiving line
- ❑ Bride and groom in receiving line
- ❑ Parents in receiving line
- ❑ Guests signing the guest book
- ❑ Buffet table
- ❑ Cake table
- ❑ Bride and groom cutting the cake
- ❑ Bride and groom feeding the cake to each other
- ❑ Bride and groom seated at the main table
- ❑ Bride and groom's first dance
- ❑ Bride dancing with her father
- ❑ Groom dancing with his mother
- ❑ Bride and groom talking with guests
- ❑ Guests dancing
- ❑ Bride and groom toasting
- ❑ Bride throwing bouquet
- ❑ Groom removing bride's garter
- ❑ Groom throwing garter
- ❑ Decorated going-away car
- ❑ Bride and groom leaving the reception

Special guests to photograph

- ❑ ____________________
- ❑ ____________________
- ❑ ____________________
- ❑ ____________________
- ❑ ____________________
- ❑ ____________________

- How many cameras does the videographer provide? A good videographer will have two cameras recording throughout the ceremony to afford the best possible views.
- Will extra lighting be provided?
- Does the videographer provide editing services? A professional may spend between 10 and 15 hours editing the video. You may also want to ask if you can keep the unedited master.
- Can the videographer do a photographic collage as part of the video?
- Does the videographer add any other special effects? What is the cost of these?
- Can you choose the music for the video?
- Does the videographer provide title screens? (Make sure you give him or her the correct spelling of everyone's names.)
- Will the videographer interview guests?
- What are the costs for the wedding package?
- How many copies will you get?
- What is the cost for additional copies?
- What are the costs for additional tape and time?
- How long will the videographer stay at the reception?

Check with your officiant to find out whether or not videography is allowed in your location. If you are having a religious ceremony, there are usually rules regarding where the videographer may set up his or her camera and whether certain portions of the ceremony are allowed to be taped.

Wedding Wisdom

A finished wedding video is usually approximately two hours long.

14
BREAK A LEG

The wedding rehearsal and rehearsal dinner usually take place the night before the wedding, but may be held up to a week before.

The wedding rehearsal is like the dress rehearsal before opening night. It's a good way to calm your nerves if you are anxious about the day. You'll run through the ceremony and have a chance to make last-minute decisions about it. It is also an opportunity to make sure that everyone in the wedding party knows what is expected of him or her.

Wedding Wisdom

Try to get an early night after the rehearsal and dinner. It's tempting to want to socialize, but you want to be as fresh as possible on your wedding day.

If possible, use the musicians who will be playing on the day. Doing so will help you accurately judge how long the service will be. The bride will also know how fast or slow the music will be as she walks down the aisle. In addition, to make things go smoothly on the day, you should practice things like passing the bouquet to the matron of honor and exchanging the rings.

Check with your officiant if your photographer can attend the wedding rehearsal. If there are restrictions on photography during the ceremony, this will be a good opportunity for the photographer and officiant to discuss when it is appropriate to take photos.

The wedding rehearsal is often followed by a rehearsal dinner. This is usually hosted by the groom's parents and may take place at a restaurant or at their home. Usually, the entire wedding party and their spouses or partners are invited, and the bride and groom may take this opportunity to present the wedding party with gifts of appreciation for their help. It's a wonderful opportunity for the wedding party to get acquainted if they do not know one another very well.

If guests from out of town have already arrived, they often appreciate being invited to the rehearsal dinner as it gives them a chance to socialize with the bride and groom. The couple are usually very busy on the wedding day and may not have much time to visit with out-of-town guests.

Use Checklist 3 to determine who will be present at the wedding rehearsal and the rehearsal dinner.

Checklist 3
Wedding Rehearsal

Location: ______________________ **Date:** ____________ **Time:** __________

Attendees:

- ❑ bride
- ❑ groom
- ❑ maid or matron of honor
- ❑ best man
- ❑ bridesmaids
- ❑ groomsmen
- ❑ flower girl
- ❑ ring bearer
- ❑ officiant
- ❑ bride's parents
- ❑ groom's parents
- ❑ videographer and photographer (optional)
- ❑ ceremony musicians/soloist
- ❑ wedding consultant
- ❑ other

____

____

____

Rehearsal dinner

Location: ______________________ **Date:** ____________ **Time:** __________

Attendees:

- ❑ bride
- ❑ groom
- ❑ maid or matron of honor
- ❑ best man
- ❑ bridesmaids
- ❑ groomsmen
- ❑ flower girl
- ❑ ring bearer
- ❑ bride's parents
- ❑ groom's parents
- ❑ other family
- ❑ out-of-town guests
- ❑ wedding party's spouses or dates
- ❑ other

____

____

____

Gifts bought for and presented to:

- ❑ maid or matron of honor
- ❑ best man
- ❑ bridesmaids
- ❑ groomsmen
- ❑ other

____

____

____

15
HAIR AND MAKEUP

Most brides choose a professional to do their wedding day makeup and hair. Not only does this ensure a polished, professional appearance on the day, but for many brides it's an opportunity for a bit of pampering on the day. And you deserve it!

Try to schedule your wedding day hair and makeup appointments at least two months before your wedding, and keep the following tips in mind so that you are relaxed and look your best on your big day.

Do —

- Keep clippings from magazines of styles and looks you like and show them to your stylist for ideas.
- Have a couple of make overs at large department stores to try out different looks.
- Have a practice session with your stylist or make-up artist (or on your own, if you're doing your own) at least a month before. Bring in a picture of your dress and take your headpiece or veil to the salon. This is often a good day to also have your bridal portrait taken.
- Have all your equipment organized if you're doing your own hair and makeup at home or at the ceremony location. Make sure there is a counter to work on and a large mirror with lots of natural light.
- Wear a button-up shirt or robe that is easy to remove without mussing up your hair or smudging your makeup.
- Have your nails manicured the day before the wedding.

Don't —

- Assume that your stylist can do extra people at the last minute. If your wedding party and family need to have their hair done, make appointments for them as well.
- Underestimate the time it takes to drive to the salon and back. Allow yourself plenty of time.
- Make drastic changes to your hair color and style on the day.
- Don't expect your usual stylist to do an intricate updo. This is best done by the resident expert.

- Burn the midnight oil in the weeks and days leading up to the wedding. A good night's sleep can be the best beauty treatment.
- Overdo the perfume. Remember to put your perfume on before you dress so that you don't stain your gown.

Your hair and makeup, however perfectly done, are likely to smudge, frizz, and frazzle a little during the course of the day. Ensure that your emergency kit contains the appropriate touch-up tools. See Checklist 4 for these and other items to pack in your emergency kit.

Checklist 4

Bride's Emergency Kit

You've taken pains to plan your wedding carefully, but some things you just can't prevent happening. If you're well prepared, though, you can keep things running smoothly in any eventuality. Have your maid/matron of honor, mother, or friend carry some of these items with her in case of an emergency:

- ❑ prescription medications
- ❑ headache, cold, and antacid medications
- ❑ feminine hygiene products
- ❑ contact lens solution/eye drops
- ❑ gum or breath mints
- ❑ band aids
- ❑ Kleenex
- ❑ pen and notepad
- ❑ compact mirror
- ❑ makeup, lipstick, nail polish, and makeup remover for clothes
- ❑ dusting powder for just before photographs are taken
- ❑ drinking straws, so you can drink while having your photo taken without messing up your lipstick
- ❑ deodorant and perfume
- ❑ nail file
- ❑ small hand towel
- ❑ gel, hairspray, hairdryer, barrettes
- ❑ toothbrush and toothpaste
- ❑ clear nail polish for runs and/or extra pantyhose
- ❑ sewing kit with the color thread of your and your bridesmaids' dresses
- ❑ safety pins and small scissors
- ❑ flat shoes if you're going to dance at the reception
- ❑ garter
- ❑ extra directions to reception
- ❑ contact numbers of all the vendors (or this guide, which contains all your important planning details)
- ❑ spare change or a cell phone
- ❑ snack food
- ❑ list of poses for photographer
- ❑ ______________________________

  ____

  ____

  ____

16
GETTING TO THE CHURCH ON TIME

Whether you choose a horse and carriage, limousine, your father's sedan, or a bicycle made for two, it is courteous to arrive at the ceremony on time. And don't overlook arranging transport to get to the reception and home again (or to the hotel or airport) afterward.

In fact, you'll probably need to make quite a few transport arrangements. The groom and his best man, groomsmen, and your parents will need to get to the ceremony in plenty of time. You'll also need transport for the bride's attendants, and probably another vehicle for the bride and her parents.

If you have your heart set on a limousine but can't afford to spring for limousines for everyone in the wedding party, consider getting one just for the bride as she arrives at the ceremony and then for the couple as they leave the ceremony. Or check out the luxury cars at your local car-rental dealership. They can be a lot more affordable than a limousine. Looking for a vintage car to set the tone for your wedding? Some private owners will rent you their car for the day. (Check in the *Yellow Pages* or with your local vintage-car club.)

> **Staying Organized**
>
> 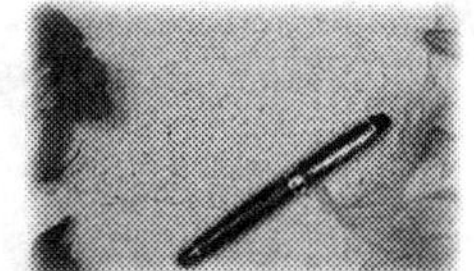
>
> *Arrange for licensed drivers for all the vehicles, and ensure that they will stay sober throughout the day so that you and your party have a safe ride home.*

If you are hiring a driver, give him or her good directions to the venue (preferably include a map). Also make sure he or she has a list of pick-up times and places and the phone numbers of the people being picked up in case of traffic or an emergency.

If many of your guests will be arriving by car, check on the parking policies of your ceremony and reception venues. You may be able to negotiate a reduced fee for your large group. And be sure to have someone reserve parking spaces near the entrance to the ceremony and the reception. If you're the bride, you'll be the last to arrive at the ceremony, and the newly-weds are often the last to arrive at the reception. You don't want to have to delay things because you couldn't find a parking space!

Use Worksheet 11 to organize the details of your wedding transportation.

Worksheet 11

Wedding Transportation

	Transport to ceremony	Pick-up time	Contact	Cost	Transport to reception	Transport home
Bride and father						
Maid of honour, bridesmaids, flower girls						
Bride and groom						
Groom and best man						
Groomsmen and ring bearer						
Bride's mother						
Groom's parents						
Other special guests						

17
THE WEDDING CEREMONY

The wedding ceremony is the moment it all happens; it's the moment you demonstrate your beliefs and pledge your commitment to each other. The format of your wedding ceremony will differ depending on the type of wedding you're having (formal or informal), your religion, and even your culture.

Where to Hold the Ceremony

Unless your religion forbids it, you don't have to get married in a place of worship. Many hotels and clubs provide altars and canopies, enabling you to hold the ceremony and reception at the same place. If you are being married by a religious representative, you should discuss these alternatives with him or her.

If you are not getting married in a place of worship, you'll need to choose a location that accommodates your needs. Book a date as early as possible if you are choosing a popular venue.

Think about some of the following when choosing the venue for your wedding ceremony:

- How many people can the location accommodate?
- If you are getting married outdoors, is there an alternate venue in case it rains?
- Are there any fees for the use of the location, the officiant, or the musicians?
- Are you allowed floral arrangements in the location?
- Are confetti, rice, or rose petals allowed to be thrown outside the location?
- Will you be able to dress at the location?
- Is an aisle carpet or canopy provided by the location?

> *Wedding Wisdom*
>
> 
>
> States and provinces have different rules regarding who can perform a legal wedding ceremony. Officiants in your state or province may include a justice of the peace, magistrate, judge, mayor, county clerk, tribal chieftain, or member of the clergy.

Civil Ceremonies

A civil wedding is one that is not performed by a member of any clergy. Most small civil weddings are performed in a courthouse, judge's chambers, city hall, or the home of the justice of the peace. For larger civil weddings, many couples choose a garden or hotel. More unique choices could include ships, parks, beaches, wineries, and historic or public sites.

A civil wedding can be quick and economical, and usually requires only two witnesses. You'll need to get a marriage license and will have to contact a marriage officer or commissioner in your area to perform the ceremony.

Civil weddings may be followed by a reception.

Religious Ceremonies

Most religions have particular rules around marriages. Talk to your officiant about some of the following if they are applicable to you:

- What is the religion's policy on remarriages?
- How does the religion handle interfaith marriages?
- What are the legal and religious requirements for witnesses (e.g., the Jewish faith requires two male witnesses, the Muslim faith requires the witnesses to be Muslim)?
- Are there any dress codes for the bridal gown or the attire of your wedding party (e.g., in certain religions the bride may be required to cover her head)?
- Do you need to attend pre-marital counselling or instructions in the faith to be married?

Even if the bride's and groom's religious backgrounds are similar, it's important to discuss the ceremony so both you and your families are comfortable with the style and format of the wedding. You should also check on any of your religion's requirements or practices. If you have different religious backgrounds, talk to both your religious representatives to see how they have handled interfaith weddings before. You may want to try combining ideas from both faiths or creating new traditions.

Planning the Ceremony

It's best to consult well in advance (usually at least six months) with your officiant when planning your ceremony. He or she will have some suggestions for the format and content of the ceremony. A traditional wedding follows more or less the following format, but yours may differ depending on personal or religious preference:

- Processional
- Hand over of bride
- Welcome to guests
- Introduction to the ceremony

- Discussion of the vows
- The exchange of rings
- Closing
- Signing of marriage certificate
- Recessional

If you're like most couples, you want your wedding ceremony to be a unique and personal event. Some couples choose to write their own vows, while others may ask a friend or family member to read a poem or sing a song that is meaningful to them. Whatever you decide to do, don't make it too complicated. You'll probably be nervous enough on the day, without having to worry about remembering poetry or lyrics. If you do decide to say or do something unique, have multiple copies of the poetry, vows, or music on hand to avoid the memory blanks that are common in the excitement of the moment.

When planning your ceremony, consider the following questions:

- How long will the ceremony be?
- Can your photographer or videographer record during the ceremony?
- If yours is an interfaith marriage, how will you accommodate each religion's rituals in the ceremony?
- Will you need to book an organist, musician, or soloist?
- Are there any restrictions on the music you select?
- Will you be allowed to compose your own vows if you want to?

Use Worksheet 12 to help you plan the format and details of your wedding ceremony.

Wedding Programs

If you are going to have a wedding program (and they do make nice souvenirs), you'll need to work with your officiant to pin down the ceremony details well in advance so that you have enough time to get the programs printed. Include the following details:

- Bride's name
- Groom's name
- Location of the ceremony
- Location of the reception
- Wedding date, ceremony time, and reception time
- Name of officiant
- Names of parents of the bride

- Names of parents of the groom
- Name of maid/matron of honor
- Name of best man
- Names of bridesmaids
- Names of groomsmen
- Name of flower girl
- Name of ring bearer
- Readers for the ceremony (you may also wish to include references to the pieces or prayers being read)
- Organist, soloist, musicians (you may also wish to include references to the musical selections)
- Order of the service (consult with your officiant for these details)
- Short messages, prayers, or poems

Worksheet 12

Wedding Ceremony

Location arrangements

Date ______________________ Time ______________

Location of ceremony ____ Fee ________________________

Contact ____ Phone ________________________________

Officiant ____ Phone ______________________ Fee ____________

Minimum no. of guests __________________________ Maximum no. of guests ________________________

Arrival time ____________________________________ Departure time ____________________________

Rehearsal date __________________________________ Rehearsal time ____________________________

Wedding programs ____

Ushers ____

Reserved seating for bride's family (left-hand side of venue):

Pew 1 ____

Pew 2 ____

Pew 3 ____

Usher: ____

Reserved seating for groom's family (right-hand side of venue):

Pew 1 ____

Pew 2 ____

Pew 3 ____

Usher: ____

Set-up time for floral arrangements ____

Person to accept gifts ____

Rice/flower petal throwers ____

Parking arrangements ____

Photography/videography restrictions ____

Cost of:

Wedding altar ____________________ Arch ______________________ Aisle stanchions ______________

Chairs __________________________ Candelabras ________________ Candles ______________________

Kneeling bench ___________________ Canopy ____________________ Other ________________________

Cleaners ____

Dressing room location ___________________________________ Available from ____________________

Ceremony format

Beginning time ______________________ End time ______________________

Readers:

Opening words ______________________ Readings ______________________

Prayers ______________________ Closing words ______________________

Changes in marriage vows ______________________

____

Music

Organist ______________________ Contact no. ______________________

Soloist ______________________ Contact no. ______________________

Other musicians ______________________

____

Fee ______________________

Special equipment needed ______________________

____

Clothing ______________________

Prelude Time to begin ______________________

Performer ______________________ Selection ______________________

First solo Time to begin ______________________

Performer ______________________ Selection ______________________

Processional Time to begin ______________________

Performer ______________________ Selection ______________________

Wedding march Time to begin ______________________

Performer ______________________ Selection ______________________

Second solo Time to begin ______________________

Performer ______________________ Selection ______________________

Additional solos

Performer(s) ______________________

Selection(s) ______________________

Time(s) to begin ______________________

Recessional Time to begin ______________________

Performer ______________________ Selection ______________________

Postlude Time to begin ______________________

Performer ______________________ Selection ______________________

Time to end: ______________________

18
THE RECEPTION

You've said your "I dos" and are officially husband and wife. It's time to show off your new status and enjoy yourselves with your family and friends. Wedding receptions range in scale from tea and cake outside the ceremony venue to dinner and dancing into the night at a nearby hotel. It all depends on the style of your wedding and your budget.

Order of Events at the Reception

The order of events at a reception may vary depending on your location, the time of day, and your personal culture, traditions, or preferences. For example, receptions are becoming more casual these days, and many couples choose to forego the receiving line.

Use the following sequence of events as a guide to planning your own reception:

- Guests gather at reception location. Guests can leave their gifts at the gift table and sign the guest book. The wedding party often has their photographs taken at another location during this time.
- Wedding party arrives and forms a receiving line. This traditionally includes the bridal couple and their parents, the best man and maid of honor, and any other special guests. This is the time when the couple can make sure that they get to greet and talk to each guest at least once. You might want to review the names of guests and their spouses a few days before the wedding to refresh your memory, especially if there are guests invited by your spouse whom you do not know.
- The master of ceremonies introduces the wedding party as they enter the reception location.
- The bride and groom take to the floor for the first dance. This may be followed by the father/daughter and mother/son dance, and then the wedding party join in, followed by the guests. Sometimes the first dance happens after the meal.
- The best man usually proposes the first toast, followed by the maid of honor, the groom's father, and the bride's father. The bridal couple or the groom may also make a speech. The best man may also read congratulatory telegrams.

Wedding Wisdom

Ask those people making toasts to limit the length of their speeches.

- While the meal is being served, the bridal couple can mingle with the guests and have the table photographs taken.
- Dancing.
- The bride and groom cut the cake for dessert. They usually cut the first slice together and may feed each other a piece as a symbol of the life they'll be sharing together. Sometimes the cutting of the cake happens directly following the toasts.
- The bouquet and garter toss.
- More dancing.
- The bridal couple leaves, followed by the guests.

Use Worksheet 13 to plan the order of events at your reception.

Getting Seated

> **Staying Organized**
>
> 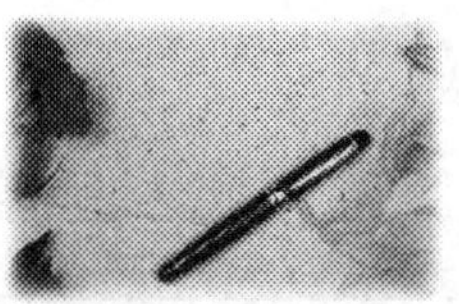
>
> Have a pen and cards available at the gift table, and ask guests to write their names on the card and tape it firmly to the gift. That way you can identify who gave what and save confusion later. If your reception is at a hotel, check that security is provided for the gift table.

If you are having a sit-down dinner or buffet for the reception, you'll need to decide how to arrange the tables and who will sit at which table. The arrangement of tables can vary depending on the formality of the wedding. The bridal couple always sits together at the head table. The head table can also include both sets of parents and other family, as well as the wedding party. It depends how much space you have and how many people are in your wedding party! Usually, there are one or two family tables near the head table.

Deciding where to seat your guests can often be a challenge. Unless you know every guest on both sides of the family very well, you may want to elicit the help of both your families to make the arrangements. Try seating people at tables at which they know at least one person. However, you could also take this opportunity to mix your families and guests a little so that they get to know people from the other side of the family.

Decide on how many people will sit at a table. Eight to ten is usually a good number. Speak to the venue coordinator. He or she will have a good idea of how best to arrange the tables in the allocated space.

One way to figure out the seating arrangements is to write each guest's name on a sticky note or 3" x 5" card, then lay them all out on the floor and move them around until you reach a satisfactory arrangement.

Once you have finalized your arrangement, post a seating chart at the door to the reception. If you want to be really specific about who takes what seat at the tables, you could put personalized place cards at each table. Otherwise, allow your guests to pick out their own seats at their designated table.

Because seating arrangements are unique to each wedding and venue, we have not provided a sample seating plan here. However, you can use Worksheet 14 to plan your own arrangement.

Worksheet 13

Order of Events at Our Reception

Event	Approx. Time	Key People Involved

Worksheet 14
Seating plan

Table # _____ Table #______ Table #______

Table # _____ Table #______ Table #______

Table # _____ Table #______ Table #______

Table # _____ Table #______ Table #______

Hiring Professional Services for Your Reception

The next few chapters of this book take you through planning a formal reception that involves dining and entertainment. Unless you are doing everything yourselves, you may find yourselves faced with having to sign a contract with a vendor (e.g., caterer, musician, or venue).

Read through the whole contract carefully and make sure that you agree with everything in it, and that nothing important has been left out. Most vendors have standard contracts that they adapt to suit the needs of each customer. If you have anything unique to your wedding that is not part of the boilerplate contract, make sure that it is added to the contract before you sign.

The contract should spell out at least the following particulars:

- *Date, time, and location of the event, as well as the full names and addresses of the vendor and yourselves.*
- *Vendor's responsibilities.* Make sure it specifies in detail who is responsible for supplying what.
- *Guarantee of guests.* The contract should specify the date by which you must let the vendor know what the final guest count will be. You will also have to make sure you have a minimum number of guests as the vendor must be able to plan accordingly.
- *The payment policies.* The contract should state when the deposit is due and how much it is, if there are any interim payments, and when the balance is due. Check whether or not the amount on the contract includes taxes and gratuities. Read through the refund and cancellation policies and make sure you are clear on how any additional expenses will be handled.
- *What licenses and permits (e.g., alcohol license, music license) are required and who is responsible for obtaining them.*
- *Whether or not the vendor is insured and whether or not you will have to take out further insurance.*

If you have any concerns about what is in the contract (or what is missing) have a lawyer look through it before signing. Remember that both you and the vendor must sign the contract, and if you make any changes to the contract, you should both initial the changes.

Use Worksheet 15 to record the contact details of all the professionals who are helping you coordinate your wedding. Take the list with you on the day of your wedding in case you urgently need to get in touch with someone.

Wedding Wisdom

If you have lots of children at your wedding, consider having a babysitter for the children's table. Their parents (and you) will certainly appreciate it. You may also want to organize goodies at their table to keep them occupied.

Staying Organized

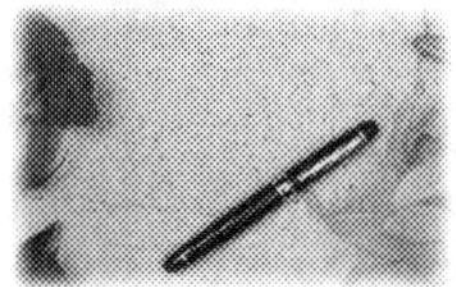

A contract of services protects both you and the vendor. It's your guarantee that the vendor will deliver as promised, and is a safeguard to the vendor that you will pay him or her for the services you've specified.

Worksheet 15

Contact List: Reception Professional Services

	Name	Contact	Address	Phone	E-mail	Deposit paid	Balance due	Set-up/ delivery time	Notes
Venue									
Caterer									
Cake									
Florist									
DJ/Band									
Limousine									
Photographer									
Videographer									
Other									

19
CHOOSING A VENUE

Some popular reception venues are booked months in advance, so this should be one of the first things you reserve after deciding on a wedding day, especially if you are tying the knot on a popular weekend.

Church halls are popular venues because of their proximity to the ceremony. They can also be relatively inexpensive to hire. Many hotels, country clubs, university clubs, and restaurants are ideal locations for receptions, and they often have staff who can help you plan your event. Beware, however, that what you gain in having experienced staff, you may lose in flexibility at these venues.

If you're looking for an outdoor location, city and state/provincial parks may provide an ideal setting, or perhaps you have a friend with a large enough home and garden who would be willing to host the reception. Home and garden weddings can offer you lots of flexibility, and are usually more personal and less expensive than renting a hall or club. However, they can involve a great deal more organizing. You'll probably have to rent equipment such as tents, chairs, tables, crockery and cutlery, and glasses, and even kitchen equipment if you plan on catering your reception yourself. Make sure you have made adequate arrangements for bathroom, lighting, and heating facilities, and check with your municipality on the parking restrictions around the house.

> **Being Budget-Wise**
>
> 
>
> *Many hotels include a bridal suite in the reception package, and may also give discounts to wedding guests staying at the hotel.*

Here are some questions to ask the co-ordinator at the reception venues you are considering:

- Have you handled a wedding reception of this size before?
- Are there any other events taking place at the same time as ours?
- What will the staff be wearing?
- Are there any extra charges?
- What is your refund/cancellation policy?

In addition, you should check on the policies regarding decorating the venue. If you are hiring a church or club hall, there may be photographs or display cabinets on the walls that you would like to cover up. Check whether the venue has drapes or tablecloths in different colors that will fit in with your color scheme. Find out if there are restrictions on the materials used for decorating and if you're allowed to light candles as part of your

Staying Organized

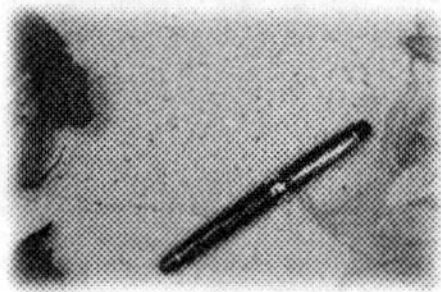

If you are planning an outdoor wedding, make alternate arrangements in case the weather turns.

The location of your reception should be large enough to accommodate the number of guests you are inviting. (And if your wedding is intimate, don't hire a large venue that will overwhelm your small party.) In addition, the venue should be easily accessible to your guests, have a dance floor (if desired), and offer a clean-up service after the reception!

centerpieces. You should also arrange to have access to the venue the day before to supervise the decorating.

Some venues offer to provide a catering service or may require you to use their own service. You may be able to negotiate a good deal if you hire the venue as well as the caterer. One benefit of this is that the caterer knows the venue well, and you'll probably have to deal only with the one vendor. On the flip side, they are probably less flexible than an independent caterer and may not be able to accommodate specific catering requirements or tastes.

Often the venue can provide the same facilities and staff (e.g., wait staff, bar staff, tablecloths, glasses, cutlery, and crockery) that a catering company can. Check out the prices and services of both the venue and your caterer before making a decision. And make sure you outline in the contract who will be providing what.

If you will be using the venue's caterer, then read Chapter 20 on choosing a caterer before booking the venue, and use the checklists in both sections to make sure you have covered all the details for both choosing a venue and choosing a caterer.

Use Worksheet 16 to organize the details of your reception venue.

Worksheet 16

Reception Venue

Location ______________________________

Contact ____________________ Phone ____________________

Headcount ____________________ Final headcount due ____________________

Cost per person ____________ Taxes ____________ Gratuity ____________

Extras (cake, cake service, staff, champagne pouring service, overtime charges) ____________

____

____

Set up and clean up included? ______________________________

Total cost ____________________ Deposit ____________________

Deposit due ____________________ Final payment due ____________________

Set up

Access to the room from ______________________________

No. of hours we have the room ______________________________

Decorations, center pieces provided? ______________________________

Smoking allowed ____________

Air conditioning ____________

Legal

_____Health license _____Liquor license _____Insurance

Catering

Linens ____________ Tables ____________ Chairs ____________

How are tables arranged? ______________________________

Silverware and serving accessories ______________________________

Cutlery ____________ Crockery ____________ Kitchen facilities ____________

No. of wait staff ____________________ No. of buffet staff ____________________

What happens to the leftovers? ______________________________

Bar

Open bar options ______________________________

Price difference for premium brands ______________________________

Charge by bottle or consumption ______________________________

Liquor provided ______________________________

____

____

Water ________________________ Ice ________________________ Soft drinks ________________________

Glasses provided? ________________________ Bar staff ________________________

Champagne ________________________ Glasses ________________________

Corkage fee? ________________________

Wedding cake

Table provided ________________________ Cutting knife provided ________________________

Cutting service provided ________________________ Extra charge? ________________________

Cake provided ________________________ Details ________________________

____

Gift table provided ________________________ Security? ________________________

Dance floor

No. of people floor can accommodate ________________________

Electrical outlets for musicians ________________________

Audio equipment provided ________________________

Lighting ________________________

Parking

Cost ________________________ Availability ________________________

Valet parking available ________________________

Coat check available ________________________

20 CHOOSING A CATERER

The easiest wedding receptions to organize simply serve wedding cake and champagne to toast the couple after the ceremony. Depending on the time of day, there may also be a buffet of cakes and pastries or cocktails — or even breakfast, if it is a morning wedding.

For afternoon and evening weddings, it is traditional to serve a meal at the reception. The meal can be prepared by a caterer or can be cooked in your own (or a friend's) kitchen. If you are doing your own catering, try to keep it simple. You want to enjoy your day, not be worrying about how the food preparation is coming along.

Some venues insist you use their own caterers. Doing so can save you time and hassle — if you are happy with what they can offer. If you use the venue's caterers, interview them the same way as you would an independent caterer. If you choose to use your own caterer, check that your venue has adequate kitchen facilities, and if possible, have your caterer visit the venue to see if it meets his or her needs.

Most caterers will charge per person, but some may offer reduced prices for children or for wedding professionals who will be attending the event (e.g., your photographer and entertainment). You'll need to guarantee that there will be a minimum number of guests attending, then confirm the actual head count by a specified date. Any changes to your guest list after that date will likely result in extra costs.

Check whether or not there are any charges additional to the per-person charge (e.g., taxes, gratuities, and overtime), and know upfront what the caterer's refund or cancellation policy is.

If you have specific dietary requirements (e.g., food must be organic, kosher, or vegetarian) be upfront with the caterer, and have the requirements written into the contract if you can. If the caterer subcontracts part of the job to other chefs or bakeries, they need to be aware of the requirements as well.

Many caterers have a number of set menus from which you can choose, but you may be able to customize the menu if you have specific preferences. Ask if the caterer provides tasting consultations at which you can sample the food he or she will be serving. The proof of a good caterer is usually in the tasting! (Check first to find out if there is a fee for the tasting consultation.)

> **Wedding Wisdom**
>
> 
>
> Ask the caterer if he or she subcontracts some of the food preparation to other bakers or chefs. This option often gives you more variety if you want exotic food at your reception. However, make sure that you are receiving the same quality food as that of the caterer you interviewed.

Finally, you may want to ask your caterer what happens to the leftover food. Some caterers will package up a meal for the bride and groom and their family to enjoy later, or you may prefer it be sent to a local shelter. (Check with the shelter regarding restrictions on the kind of food they can accept. Some shelters cannot accept perishable items.) However, if you don't specify what you want done with any remaining food, you may find that the caterer literally "cleans up," and the leftover food could disappear into the garbage!

Use Worksheet 17 to organize the details of having your reception catered.

Worksheet 17

Caterer

Company ______________________________

Contact ______________________ Phone ______________________

Location ______________________ Time ______________________

Directions to location ______________________________

____

Indoors or outdoors ______________________________

Head count ______________________ Final head count due ______________________

Cost per person ______________ Taxes ______________ Gratuity ______________

Extras (cake, cake service, staff, champagne pouring service, overtime charges) ______________

____

____

Set-up and clean-up included? ______________________________

Total cost ______________________ Deposit ______________________

Deposit due ______________________ Final payment due ______________________

Legal

_____ Health license _____ Liquor license _____ Insurance

Set up

Arrival time ______________________ Hours of service ______________________

Equipment provided ______________________________

Kitchen facilities needed (e.g., ovens, refrigerators, BBQs) ______________________

____

____

Decorations, centre pieces provided? ______________________________

Linens ______________ Tables ______________ Chairs ______________

How are tables arranged? ______________________________

Silverware and serving accessories ______________________________

No. of wait staff ______________________ No. of buffet staff ______________________

Staff dress code ______________________________

Serving times

Cocktails ______________ Main course ______________ Dessert or cake ______________

Type of service

Cocktails: Passed around or stationary ______

Main course: Formal sit-down or buffet ______

Dessert ______

Menu

Cocktails ______

______

Main course ______

______

______

______

Salads ______

______

______

Side dishes ______

______

Breads ______

Dessert ______

______

Wedding cake

Table provided ______ Cutting knife provided ______

Cutting service provided ______ Extra charge? ______

Cake provided ______ Details ______

______

21
THE BAR

Whether the venue or the caterer is handling the bar, make sure you establish strict policies around alcohol. This is one area in which costs can quickly escalate and can easily break even the most carefully managed budget.

Even the smallest reception has at least champagne to toast the bride and groom. Whether or not you serve other alcohol is up to you. Ask your caterer for advice on the average number of drinks per guest. Unless your friends and family drink a lot more or less than average, caterers can give you a fairly accurate estimate based on their experience.

If the venue or caterer is providing the alcohol, find out what brand they serve. You may be able to negotiate changing the brand to one you prefer. You'll also need to know what they charge per drink. One way to save money on the alcohol is to ask if you can supply your own and then to buy from a wholesaler. Beware, though, that many venues or caterers will charge a corkage fee if you supply your own alcohol.

Keep careful control over the alcohol inventory and consider asking a friend to keep an eye on the bartenders. The best way to do this is to keep a list of the alcohol ordered before the reception, and then to count both opened and unopened bottles after the reception to see if they tally. Use Worksheet 18 to keep track.

Remember that not everyone drinks alcohol, so have non-alcoholic drinks available, as well as tea and coffee. Also consider assigning designated drivers to make sure all your guests arrive home safely.

Staying Organized

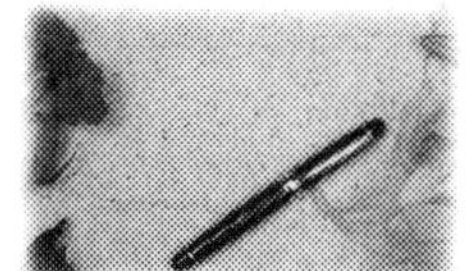

Check that the venue or caterer has the required liquor license to serve liquor at your reception.

Worksheet 18

Bar

Number of guests ____________

Liquor ordered	Brand	Quantity at start	End: Opened	End: Unopened	Cost per item	Total cost
Champagne						
Bourbon						
Gin						
Rum						
Scotch						
Vermouth						
Vodka						
Red wine						
White wine						
Punch						
Beer						
Beer						
Beer						
Liqueur						
Liqueur						
Soft drinks						
Soft drinks						
Soft drinks						
Other						
Other						
Other						
Tea						
Coffee						

22
HAVING YOUR CAKE

Many caterers will provide a wedding cake either as part of their package or for an additional charge. Alternatively, you may want to hire an independent baker or ask a talented friend to make your cake. The cake is usually on display on a separate table during the reception. Check with your caterer or the venue coordinator if a cake table and cutting knife are provided as part of the package.

The bride and groom usually cut the first slice of cake and feed it to each other as a symbol of the life they will be sharing together. You'll probably need someone knowledgeable to cut the cake after the bride and groom have cut the first slice, as cutting a tiered cake is challenging. Ask your caterer if he or she provides a cutting service as part of the package or if there is an extra charge. If you are having a baker provide the cake, he or she will often give instruction on how to cut it.

> **Wedding Wisdom**
>
> 
>
> *The top layer of the cake is traditionally saved for your first anniversary. Cover the top layer and freeze it overnight. Then, seal the cake in plastic wrap and place it in an airtight container before freezing.*

Cake Styles

Wedding cakes come in a variety of shapes, textures, and tastes. You can't please everyone, but if you are having a tiered cake, you might consider making each tier a different flavor. Your baker will suggest some flavor options, and you should ask if you can do a taste test.

If you're having a theme wedding, the wedding cake is a wonderful place to start. You can choose a color and decorations or embellishments that match your theme. Avoid decorating with fresh flowers, however, unless you are positive that they have not been sprayed with pesticides.

Use Worksheet 19 to help you stay on track with your cake.

Worksheet 19

Wedding Cake

Table provided at venue ____________________

Table decorations ____________________

Cutting knife provided ____________________

Cutting service provided ____________________ Extra charge? ____________________

Baker ____________________ Contact ____________________

Phone ____________________ Cost ____________________

Extra cost for delivery/cutting ____________________

Delivery of cake to reception ____________________

Directions given to reception ____________________

____

No. of guests ____________________ No. of slices ____________________

Flavor ____________________

Icing ____________________

Style ____________________

Decorations ____________________

____

Colors ____________________

23
AND THE BAND PLAYED ON

The music you choose sets the tone for your wedding. As well as creating an atmosphere for the reception, it also reflects the married couple's personality.

You can splash for a live band or hire a disc jockey to play recorded music. Many bands or DJs will also act as the master of ceremonies, but check if they need any special microphone equipment to do this. Choose your entertainment carefully: their personalities can help (or hinder) the mood at your reception.

Staying Organized

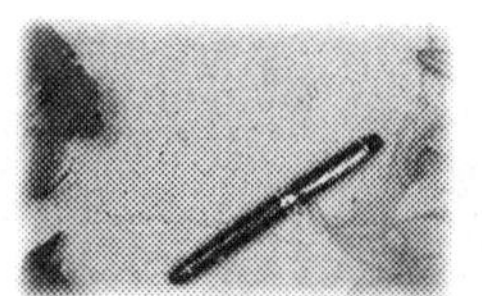

Check out what the musicians will wear to the reception. If you have a theme or color scheme, see if they can match it.

Choosing a Music Style

Some wedding bands have an audition night during which you can hear them play, or they may be featured at your local bridal show. You can also ask for audio or video tapes. Perhaps you heard a great DJ at a friend's wedding or have a favorite band from a club. Just be sure that they can play music that suits your tastes and style, as well as that of your friends and family.

A good wedding band should be versatile and be able to play a wide selection of styles, from background music during cocktails and dinner to dance music once the party begins. Discuss the style or theme of your wedding with your musicians or DJ. Let them know whether you want the reception to have a fun, party atmosphere with lots of audience involvement, or if it should be a quieter affair that gives you lots of time to visit with your guests.

Professional wedding musicians will usually ask you the age range of the guests attending so that they can get some idea of the selection of music they should play. Try to give the musicians a timeline of events so that they can plan the music and their breaks. You could also specify a favorite piece of music for the bride and groom's first dance, and any other special requests. Find out whether the musicians take requests from the floor.

Staying Organized

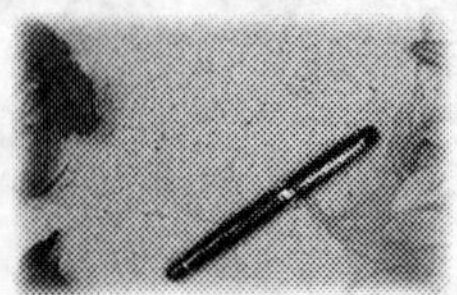

Find out whether or not the band arranges for background music to be played while they are taking their breaks.

The Contract

As with any other vendor, discuss with your musicians or DJ all details of payment upfront and note their refund and cancellation policies. Most venues require musicians to have liability insurance, and if you are using a disc jockey in Canada, check whether his or her business is registered with the Audio Video Licensing Agency (AVLA) to legally play re-recorded music. You may also want to check their standing with the Better Business Bureau.

If the musicians need any special equipment, this should be noted in the contract so that there are no surprises when they set up. You'll need to arrange access to the venue so that they can set up well before the reception begins, and be clear on when their obligation ends (and on what the overtime charges are). You don't want the musicians to be packing up just as soon as the party gets going.

Use Worksheet 20 to organize the music for your reception.

Worksheet 20

Musicians

Band/DJ ______________________________

Contact ______________________ Phone ______________________

Act as master of ceremonies? ______________________________

Wireless microphone/public address system provided? ______________________

Lighting and other special effects provided? ______________________

Cost ______________ Taxes ______________ Gratuity ______________

Additional costs ______________________________

Total costs ______________________________

Deposit ______________________ Deposit due ______________________

Overtime charges ______________________________

Number of breaks ______________________________

Directions to venue ______________________________

____

Set-up time (at least 2 hours before guests arrive) ______________________

Parking arranged for set-up ______________________________

End time ______________

Special equipment needed ______________________________

Storage for equipment ______________________________

Dressing room location ______________________________

Musical requests

First dance ______________________________

Other special requests ______________________________

____

____

____

____

____

Reception timeline ______________________________

____

____

____

____

____

24
THE HONEYMOON

Don't let your preparations for your wedding day overshadow your honeymoon. Your honeymoon should be a getaway of a lifetime — whether you're traveling to a paradise island or spending a relaxing weekend out of the city. You deserve a break for just the two of you to celebrate your marriage.

It's never too early to start planning. Traditionally, honeymoon preparations were the domain of the groom, but today most couples plan this special trip together. Planning is key to making this a special time.

Wedding Wisdom

If you're not leaving for your destination immediately after the wedding, reserve a night in a hotel with a wedding suite: it's the perfect way to end a perfect day.

Many couples hop on a plane for their honeymoon directly after the wedding reception. Others will leave a few days later, choosing to spend time after the wedding with friends and family (who have perhaps traveled from out of town for the occasion). Still others may postpone their honeymoon for a few weeks or months after the wedding.

If you're leaving directly after the reception for your honeymoon, your destination could dictate the time of year and date of your wedding. Speak to a knowledgeable travel agent about the availability of flights to and accommodation at your destination. You may also want to plan around low season times to keep the trip affordable.

Keep these tips in mind when talking to your travel agent:

- Book an early morning flight, rather than an evening flight directly after your reception. That way you can be sure that you'll have all your packing done in time and you can relax and enjoy every minute of your wedding reception.
- If you're looking to relax, consider going to an all-inclusive resort that takes care of all the details. Check with your travel agent, though, that the destination you choose is aimed at couples your age.
- Allow yourselves time to relax on your trip. If you pack every minute of your itinerary with an activity, you won't have time to unwind with your new spouse or congratulate yourselves on pulling off the wedding of the year!
- Don't forget to buy travel and medical insurance; otherwise, your trip of a lifetime could turn into a disaster.
- When planning your honeymoon, use Checklist 5 to keep track of all the essentials.

Checklist 5
Honeymoon Essentials

What you pack will depend on where you're heading. But don't forget these essentials in your luggage (and remember to label your luggage with your name and contact details):

- ❑ Passport
- ❑ Visas
- ❑ Airline tickets
- ❑ Itinerary
- ❑ Reservation information (car rentals, accommodation)
- ❑ Emergency contact information
- ❑ Traveler's checks
- ❑ Medication
- ❑ Change of clothing in your carry-on luggage
- ❑ Keys for luggage, car, and house
- ❑ Raincoat/umbrella
- ❑ Toiletries
- ❑ Contacts and contact solution
- ❑ Eye glasses and repair kit
- ❑ Sun glasses
- ❑ Sunblock and after-sun lotion
- ❑ Insect repellent
- ❑ Camera and film/batteries
- ❑ Alarm clock
- ❑ Binoculars
- ❑ First aid kit
- ❑ Maps

Staying Organized

Leave your destination plans with a trusted friend or family member in case of an emergency.

Honeymoon Registry Services

If you already have everything you need for your home and feel you don't need a traditional wedding registry, why not try a honeymoon registry? A honeymoon registry can enable a couple to have the honeymoon of their dreams, or simply the little extras that they may not have been able to afford on their trip. It also allows family and friends to contribute a meaningful gift to the couple that will remain in their memories forever.

Once you have planned your trip, the honeymoon registry creates a list of items (much like a department store bridal registry) for which guests can either fully pay or can contribute toward. The list could include any of the following things:

- Airfare
- Nightly accommodation
- Special dinners or meals
- Activities at the destination, such as a scuba diving lesson, entrance to a theme park or museum, or tickets to shows

There are companies that specialize in honeymoon registries, although some travel agencies may also offer a limited service. Limited service registries simply allow guests to mail in their checks. Some may not even give guests the option of specifying the item or activity toward which their contribution will go. Full-service registries, however, provide guests with a list of activities and items and their corresponding costs, allowing friends and family to feel that they are contributing something meaningful to your honeymoon.

Many registries will take care of distributing the list to friends and family (either by mail or on the Internet) and will have a toll-free number to make it easier for out-of-town guests to contribute. They will also provide guests with a gift certificate and receipt so that they can present it to the couple, and so that you can keep track of who contributed what when it comes time to write those thank-yous.

25
LEGALITIES

Pre-Nuptial Agreements

Depending on your personal and financial situation, you may decide to ask a lawyer to draw up a pre-nuptial or pre-marital agreement before your wedding ceremony. Although the agreement is signed before the wedding, it becomes effective only once you are married.

Such agreements may deal with financial aspects of a couple's married life, but they most commonly outline arrangements should you separate or get divorced. In such cases, a pre-marital agreement can often safeguard inheritances and some earnings from becoming part of the divorce settlement. The agreement can also make arrangements regarding children of a previous marriage.

While a pre-marital agreement can outline your and your fiancé's wishes, remember that the divorce legislation in your state or province may overrule a pre-marital agreement if the agreement appears to unfairly place one spouse in financial hardship. Your lawyer is the best person to advise you on whether or not a pre-nuptial agreement is necessary in your case.

For more information, consult *Living Together Contract,* another title published by Self-Counsel Press.

> **Wedding Wisdom**
>
> 
>
> *If you are signing a pre-nuptial agreement, make sure that you and you fiancé both get independent legal advice.*

Getting a Marriage License

Each state and province has its own rules regarding marriage licenses. Some will allow you to get married on the same day as you get the license; others have a waiting period. Most marriage licenses have an expiry date and some may be valid only in certain jurisdictions.

Call your county clerk or local municipality to find out who issues licenses in your area and to see if you need to set up an appointment. Often you and your fiancé will have to apply together in person. Also check what you will need to bring with you. You may also need —

- proof of residency or citizenship,

- proof of age (if you are under the age of majority, you may need special permission to marry),
- a health certificate,
- proof of divorce (if applicable),
- the fee for the license, and
- your parents' names, their maiden names, and the places and dates of their birth

Check to see where the license is valid. You will probably have to get a license in the jurisdiction in which you wish to get married. Also check whether your home jurisdiction recognizes the marriage license as a legal marriage.

Registering the Marriage

After the marriage ceremony, your officiant will help you complete a marriage registration form. He or she will send it (usually within 48 hours) to the vital statistics agency in your state or province, where the marriage is registered and a legal record is kept.

On the day of the ceremony, your officiant will usually give you an interim statement of marriage document that you can use temporarily to prove that you were married. You will receive a permanent marriage certificate from the vital statistics agency once they have received the marriage registration form. Keep this certificate in a safe place. If you are changing your name (see below), you will need to show this certificate as proof of your legal marriage.

Your Rights and Responsibilities under the Law

Congratulations. You've gotten hitched, you've tied the knot, you're joined at the hip. Well, not quite joined at the hip, but now that you are a married couple in the eyes of the law, you have certain rights and responsibilities. Under the law you —

- become a beneficiary of your spouse's estate should he or she die without a will;
- file joint income taxes with the IRS or Canada Customs and Revenue Agency;
- can receive spouses' and dependants' Social Security, disability, unemployment, veterans' pension, and public assistance benefits;
- can sue another person for the wrongful death of your spouse;
- may be able to receive family rates for medical and property insurance; and
- can make medical decisions about the health of your spouse if he or she is incapacitated.

Will

Your will becomes null and void once you have married, so it's important to have it changed. It's best to visit your lawyer a few weeks before your wedding to do this in anticipation of your marriage. Take this opportunity to update any other bequests or information in your will. Once you have completed the will, give a copy to your executor, and keep a copy for yourself in a safe place. Remember to update the will if your situation changes; for example, if you have children or if your financial situation changes. For more information, see *Wills Guide for America* or *Wills Guide for Canada*, both published by Self-Counsel Press.

Changing Your Name

Traditionally, after getting married, the new bride would take her husband's surname. While many women still follow this tradition, some choose other options:

- They may keep their maiden names.
- The couple (or one spouse only) may choose a hyphenated surname, with either surname appearing first.
- Some women choose to keep their maiden names to preserve their professional identity, but use their married names for their personal identity.

Every jurisdiction has different rules regarding the legal effect of a name change. In most states and provinces, choosing to change your name to your spouse's name does not result in a legal change of name, or in any automatic change to birth records. You can decide to return to your own surname at any time. If you choose to use a hyphenated surname as your legal name, you will likely have to file a legal Change of Name document in your state or province. Check with your local government on the rules in your jurisdiction.

Remember to use your new name consistently on all legal documents. Use Checklist 6 to ensure you have changed your name on all your important documents.

Checklist 6

Change of Name

If you are changing your name, be sure to use it consistently on the following documents and with the following agencies.

- ❑ Driver's license
- ❑ Social Security card or Social Identity card
- ❑ Internal Revenue Service or Canada Customs and Revenue Agency
- ❑ Bank accounts and investments
- ❑ Insurance policies
- ❑ Property ownership documents (e.g., vehicle certificates of ownership, property titles of deed)
- ❑ Credit cards and lines of credit
- ❑ Voter's registration
- ❑ Medical records
- ❑ Passports
- ❑ Pension plans
- ❑ Subscriptions
- ❑ Employer and school records